North Sea Battleground
The War at Sea 1914–18

North Sea Battleground
The War at Sea 1914–18

by

Bryan Perrett

Pen & Sword
MARITIME

First published in Great Britain in 2011 by
Pen & Sword Maritime
an imprint of
Pen & Sword Books Ltd
47 Church Street
Barnsley
South Yorkshire
S70 2AS

ISBN: 978-1-84884-450-6

A CIP catalogue record for this book is
available from the British Library.

Typeset in 12/13.5pt Palatino by
Concept, Huddersfield, West Yorkshire

Printed and bound in England by
CPI UK

Pen & Sword Books Ltd incorporates the Imprints of Pen & Sword
Aviation, Pen & Sword Family History, Pen & Sword Maritime, Pen &
Sword Military, Pen & Sword Discovery, Wharncliffe Local History,
Wharncliffe True Crime, Wharncliffe Transport, Pen & Sword Select,
Pen & Sword Military Classics, Leo Cooper, The Praetorian Press,
Remember When, Seaforth Publishing and Frontline Publishing.

For a complete list of Pen & Sword titles please contact
PEN & SWORD BOOKS LIMITED
47 Church Street, Barnsley, South Yorkshire, S70 2AS, England
E-mail: enquiries@pen-and-sword.co.uk
Website: www.pen-and-sword.co.uk

Contents

Chapter 1   Introduction   1

Chapter 2   The Warlord   11

Chapter 3   Kicking in the Front Door – The Battle of Heligoland Bight   17

Chapter 4   Off to Yarmouth for the Day   25

Chapter 5   Admiral Ingenohl Decides to Go Home   31

Chapter 6   Dawn Bombardment – The German Bombardments of Scarborough, Whitby and Hartlepool   43

Chapter 7   Once Too Often – The Battle of Dogger Bank   63

Chapter 8   Scheer Strikes Back   71

Chapter 9   Strafing the Island (1)   79

Chapter 10   A Battle Long Awaited – Jutland and Its Sequel   91

Chapter 11   Strafing the Island (2)   105

Chapter 12   North and South – Destroyer Actions, Attacks on Scandinavian Convoys, Second Battle of Heligoland Bight   111

Chapter 13 End Game – The Zeebrugge and Ostend
            Raids   125

Chapter 14 Envoie – The End of the High Seas Fleet
            – Mutiny, Internment and Scuttling   137

Appendix   The Admirals   143
Bibliography   149
Index   150

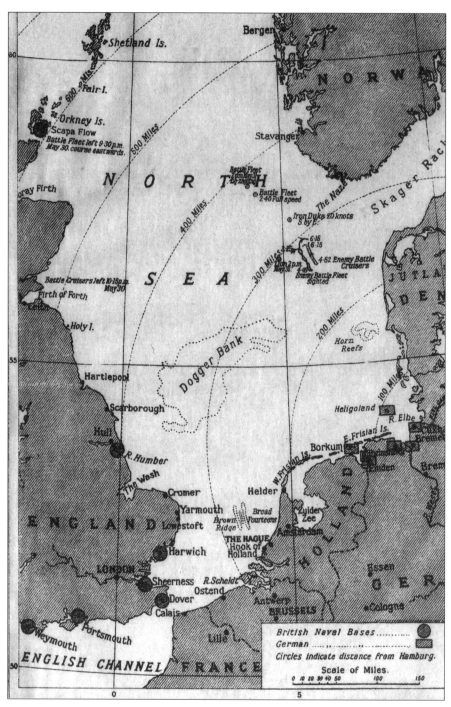

Map 1. This chart shows the major British and German naval bases within the area covered by this book. It also includes some details concerning the Battle of Jutland.

CHAPTER 1

Introduction

In 1914 it was fully understood by Germany's higher naval and military authorities that, despite having acquired the largest empire in the world, the civilian population of the British Isles had not experienced war at first hand since the Civil Wars of the mid-17th Century, save for brief and mainly local hostilities resulting from the Jacobite risings, an abortive French landing at Fishguard in 1797, and an equally abortive rising, with French support, in Ireland the following year. This was considered to be an area of general weakness that could be exploited with the object of eroding the British will to continue fighting.

This exploitation, it was believed, could be achieved in a number of ways. First, while a general engagement between the German High Seas Fleet and the British Grand Fleet would probably end in victory for the latter on the basis of size alone, a series of raids along the UK's East Coast would erode the confidence of the British public in the Royal Navy's ability to provide the same degree of protection that existed throughout the Napoleonic Wars. This would be aggravated by the Grand Fleet having been deployed to Scapa Flow in the extreme north, leaving large areas of the east coast protected by light naval units that could easily be overwhelmed at the point of contact. Civilian casualties incurred in this kind of raid would generate a sense of unease along the coast, together with the fear of a German landing in pursuit of local objectives.

Second, air power could be deployed to generate further unease inland. Naval Zeppelin airships were already performing reconnaissance duties for the High Seas Fleet and, together with the Army's Zeppelins, these could be armed with bombs and attack wide areas of the British mainland. It was true that the weight of munitions carried by the Zeppelins was only a fraction of that carried by, say, a battle cruiser, but the sheer unpredictability of raids that inflicted death, injury and destruction across a wide area would, it was believed, further damage British morale. The only property exempted from attack was that belonging to the Royal Family, by personal order of the Kaiser. Furthermore, to provide a defence against the Zeppelins, the British authorities would have to retain at home thousands of men plus hundreds of guns and aircraft that could have been put to good use on the Western Front.

Much would depend on control of the North Sea. In this respect the British demonstrated an early superiority by carrying out a destructive raid into the Heligoland Bight, on the very doorstep of the High Seas Fleet. This resulted in several German cruisers being sunk at little cost to the Royal Navy. For their part, the Germans had to accept that naval attacks on the British mainland had to be hit-and-run affairs, conducted before the battleships and battle cruisers of the Grand Fleet could be brought south to deal with the attackers. In this respect, the Germans, little knowing that copies of their signal code books had fallen into British hands, were in for a most unpleasant surprise. Somehow, with the exception of the first raid, which simply resulted in a pointless bombardment of the Yarmouth foreshore and the loss of a German armoured cruiser in a minefield, the Royal Navy seemed to have an uncanny habit of appearing in strength whenever a raid was in progress. The raids on Scarborough, Whitby and the Hartlepools in December 1914 were at first considered to be a brilliant success, but subsequent analysis proved that they had been counter-productive. First, they involved heavy loss of civilian life although no military installations existed at Scarborough or Whitby. This wanton targeting of innocent civilians not only provided a spur to British recruiting, which was already good, but also earned the condemnation of neutral powers. Further examination revealed that thanks to a combination of poor visibility and sheer luck, the raiders escaped by the skin of their teeth. The following month a sortie to the Dogger Bank area resulted in a battle that ended with the loss of a heavy cruiser. The Kaiser was furious. It would be over a year before he sanctioned another foray by heavy units of his surface fleet and that ended in serious mine damage to one of his precious battle cruisers to little purpose.

Meanwhile, the Zeppelin air offensive had started on the night of 19–20 January 1915 and gradually gathered pace throughout the year, involving naval and to a lesser extent Army airships. A small number of raids inflicted serious civilian casualties and damage, but most produced trivial results for the effort involved. The initial reaction was one of anger that the Royal Navy had permitted the raiders to get through. This was quickly followed by a realisation that there was little that the surface fleet could do to prevent Zeppelin raids and an acceptance that the Germans possessed air superiority over large areas of the North Sea. However, once initial fears of wholesale death and destruction raining from the skies proved to be unfounded, public attitudes hardened. After the North Sea bombardments the general opinion was that this sort of cowardly attack on defenceless civilians was all that could be expected from the enemy. More subtle was the change brought about by the ever-lengthening casualty lists from the front, lists that would grow longer still and leave barely a family in the land untouched. For the first time the general public felt that they were as much part of the war as the citizen soldiers fighting in the trenches, so that instead of civilian morale cracking as a result of the air attacks, it actually hardened.

The only real effect the raids had on the British war effort was the unwelcome diversion of numerous Royal Flying Corps and Royal Naval Air Service fighter squadrons to home defence, together with the creation of a substantial anti-aircraft defence organisation including early warning and ground control systems, anti-aircraft artillery batteries and searchlight units. To some extent this was made easier by the fact that the airships' most favoured targets were situated in London and south-eastern England. This meant that they entered British airspace over East Anglia and, having completed their mission, left via Kent or Essex. It was easy, therefore, to construct defensive cordons across the entry and exit routes.

At first the Zeppelins seemed invulnerable because they could reach greater heights than the fighter aircraft in service. Even if a fighter was able to engage at the same height, conventional machine gun bullets simply created punctures in the gasbags that could be sealed easily with patches. When better aircraft entered service they were sometimes able to operate above the Zeppelins and could inflict fatal damage by dropping small high explosive bombs or explosive darts on the envelope, starting fires that the airships could not control and which guaranteed most of their crews a horrible death. With the introduction of incendiary and explosive bullets, perfected by the fireworks industry, it became possible for a fighter to carry out a successful attack not only from above, but also from the side and below. Anti-aircraft fire also claimed a number of kills.

There were also a number of problems inherent in Zeppelin operations. Any significant wind pushed the huge bulk and light weight of the airships about and made them difficult to navigate if landmarks were not visible. The airships were also extremely flimsy, so that bad handling in their hangars or a heavy landing could involve their being damaged beyond repair. Occasionally, Zeppelins damaged in action would be forced to ditch in the North Sea or on the coasts of neutral Denmark or Holland. By the end of 1916 even Count Zeppelin recognised that the number of losses caused by enemy action and other accidents made their continued use prohibitively expensive in relation to the damage they caused. As described below, from that point onwards the air offensive against the United Kingdom was progressively taken up by heavier-than-air bombers.

Meanwhile, though not directly relevant to operations in the North Sea, the Imperial German Navy had embarked on a campaign of unrestricted submarine warfare. The sinking of the luxury liner *Lusitania* on 7 May 1915 off the southern coast of Ireland with the loss of 1,198 lives, including 128 Americans, caused widespread international protests which the Germans ignored. On 19 August the small *Arabic* was torpedoed and sunk with the loss of 40 lives, including three Americans. This also generated angry protests, causing the Germans to abandon submerged attacks. On 24 March 1916 the sinking of the French cross-Channel ferry *Sussex*, with some loss of life, led to such furious American protests that the policy was temporarily abandoned.

In May 1916 the German High Seas Fleet, under the command of Admiral Reinhard Scheer, reverted to the strategy of trying to ambush a portion of the British Grand Fleet. The result was the Battle of Jutland, fought in bad visibility during the afternoon and night of 31 May–1 June. The British loss in ships and men was the heavier but it was the High Seas Fleet that fled to its harbours in critically damaged condition. On the basis of statistics, the German press claimed a victory, while British reports of the action were largely negative in their tone. The British public had been looking forward to a victory on the scale of Trafalgar and, following in the wake of the Royal Navy's failure to force the Dardanelles the previous year and the enemy attacks on the coast, it was bitterly disappointed. This sense of gloom deepened when, on 5 June, Field Marshal Lord Kitchener was drowned when the cruiser *Hampshire*, in which he was travelling to Russia, struck a mine and sank off the Orkneys. The depression produced by these events failed to take into account the fact that Jellicoe was able to take the Grand Fleet to sea within days of the battle, whereas the High Seas Fleet remained incapable of fighting for many weeks. Indeed, informed opinion in Germany recognised that another such 'victory' would be disastrous.

Not until 19 August was Scheer able to take the High Seas Fleet to sea again, but Jellicoe, forewarned as usual, was already bearing down on him with the entire Grand Fleet before he had fully cleared harbour. Once at sea a false Zeppelin report of a smaller British presence to the south caused Scheer to veer away in that direction, thereby inadvertently avoiding what would almost certainly have been a serious defeat for the Germans. Significantly, this was the last occasion on which Scheer was permitted to incorporate Zeppelins and U-boats in his fleet operations.

On 3 November 1916 Scheer despatched six of his dreadnought battleships to the rescue of two stranded U-boats, only to have two of them torpedoed by British submarines. This would be the last occasion on which German capital ships entered the North Sea until April 1918. During that period the fleet's morale began to rot as it remained in harbour and many of its men transferred to the U-boat arm, which was producing good results further afield. One curious result of this constant inactivity on Scheer's part made Jellicoe suspicious of enemy traps and he confined the Grand Fleet's operations to the north of latitude 55 degrees 30 minutes. For the moment, therefore, neither fleet engaged in active operations in the North Sea.

For both sides, the pattern of operations now involved much smaller forces and centred on the north-eastern and south-western areas of the North Sea. The German Army's advances of 1914 had left it in possession of most of the Belgian coast, including the ports of Ostend and Zeebrugge, from both of which canals ran inland to the dockyard facilities of Bruges. This area was developed into a base for

U-boats and destroyers. On 26/27 October 1916 no less than 24 German destroyers, released from the need to screen the larger warships, penetrated as far south as Folkestone, bombarded the coast, sank a destroyer, an empty troop transport and six drifters, and seriously menaced British cross-Channel communications with France, all without loss. As John Buchan commented in his history of the war, 'The wonder was not that it had happened, but that it had not happened before.' This German success was offset by the loss of seven out of eleven destroyers in a Russian minefield in the Baltic on the night of 9/10 November 1916.

On 17 March 1917 a further German raid into the Channel was foiled by the destroyer *Broke*, under Commander E.R.G.R. Evans, which sank two of her opponents in a sea fight reminiscent of the Nelson touch. In May and June Ostend and Zeebrugge were bombarded. Some damage was caused, but the ports continued to be used by U-boats and destroyers. On 15 July a sortie sank or captured German merchant shipping off the Dutch coast. Scheer, however, decided to exploit the fact that some British convoys, especially those to and from Scandinavia, were lightly escorted. On 17 October two German cruisers sank most of the merchant ships in one of these as well as two escorting destroyers, some 65 miles east of Lerwick. Off the German coast, constant activity by minesweepers was necessary to keep the approaches to the U-boat bases clear. On 17 November this led to the inconclusive Second Battle of Heligoland Bight in which the British sustained damage and the Germans lost a minesweeper. On 12 December four German destroyers all but wiped out another Scandinavian convoy. As a result of this, these convoys were subsequently escorted by a squadron of battleships which the Grand Fleet was able to spare after its strength had been reinforced by the arrival of an American contingent.

In the wider sphere, the Allied blockade had begun to bite deep into every aspect of life within Germany. It was believed by the German High Command that its effects

could only get worse and that the risks involved in permitting U-boats to return to unrestricted attacks, governed
only by the Prize Rules, were justified. It was felt that even
if America entered the war, the United Kingdom could be
starved into submission long before she could make a significant contribution. The strategy proved to be so successful
that at one period Great Britain had only a few months'
supplies in hand. The situation improved dramatically when,
finally, the Admiralty introduced escorted convoys for all
sailings in addition to those bound to and from Scandinavia.
As an additional precaution, escorted convoys frequently
used routes that differed from the existing shipping lanes,
while the recently developed depth charge proved to be a
decisive anti-submarine weapon. Elsewhere, the German air
offensive continued throughout 1917 with most of the effort
being made by Gotha heavy bombers. This failed to have the
decisive impact that had been hoped for as the British anti-
aircraft and fighter defences improved steadily.

Overall, however, the year 1917 had not been a happy
one for the Allies. The Passchendaele offensive had repeated
the slaughter of the Somme, although the development of
the tank seemed to offer grounds for hope. Russia had been
knocked out of the war, the French Army was recovering
slowly from the disastrous Nivelle offensive and it would
be months before the United States could play a major role
on the battlefield. Despite the introduction of conscription,
the United Kingdom was reaching the end of its manpower resources. There were also acute shortages and price
inflation. There seemed to be no end to the war in sight
and serious concern as to what would happen when those
German divisions released by the collapse of Russia reached
the Western Front. Ironically, the first cracks in the enemy's
morale began to appear among the crew of the High Seas
Fleet.

Between March and July 1918 repeated German offensives
on the Western Front narrowly failed to break the Allied line.
The Germans leadership had unwisely promised its troops

victory and when it failed to appear, despite the willing sacrifices that had been made, trust in their leaders began to crumble. From the time of the British massed tank attack at Amiens on 8 August the German Army was in constant retreat.

In the North Sea a major raid was mounted against German bases of Zeebrugge and Ostend on 23 April with the intention of closing the entrances of the Bruges canals with blockships. The raid was only a limited success but was remarkable for the courage with which it was carried out. That against Ostend was repeated on 10 May. German morale was lowered by the British ability to carry out such heavy raids against their vulnerable seaward flank while their own offensives were in progress. Although the canal mouths were re-opened quickly, the two ports were evacuated in conformity with the German Army's general retreat and several U-boats and destroyers under repair had to be left behind.

For a variety of reasons that will be described in detail, the High Seas Fleet, once the Kaiser's pride and joy, refused to fight one final battle and mutinied, thereby provoking a revolution throughout Germany. On 21 November 1918 the major part of its strength sailed across the North Sea under humiliating escort, first to the Firth of Forth and then to Scapa Flow, where it scuttled itself seven months later.

CHAPTER 2

The Warlord

Prinz Friedrich Wilhelm Viktor Hohenzollern von Preussen, the future Kaiser Wilhelm II, first saw the light of day on 27th January 1859. It was a difficult breech birth resulting in Erbs Palsey and it left him with a withered left arm. In later life he was able to conceal this disability by resting his left hand on his sword hilt or bridle if mounted, or by using it to carry a pair of white gloves or a cane to produce a fair impression of normality. It was also said that during his birth the supply of blood to the brain was interrupted for a period and this may have contributed to his erratic, impulsive and self-contradictory personality.

For example, he was the first grandchild of the British Queen Victoria, whom he dearly loved and deeply mourned when she died. His mother, also named Victoria, had been the United Kingdom's Princess Royal, although his feelings for her were very different. His father inherited the throne to become Kaiser Friedrich III, Germany's second Emperor, but he reigned for only 99 days. Wilhelm's view of these events was summed up in one unjustifiable and hysterical outburst: 'An English doctor killed my father and an English doctor crippled my arm, which is the fault of my mother!' Who, of course, also happened to be English.

Wilhelm fitted perfectly into the militaristic society which was the Germany of the time. Depending upon any one day's programme, he might change into different uniforms every few hours, requiring considerable forethought and activity on the part of his servants, all of which seemed quite unremarkable for the Supreme Commander of mainland Europe's most efficient army. Parades, reviews and manoeuvres all enabled him to posture to his heart's content, assisted by a distinctive turned-up moustache producing an impression of ferocity. Those with some knowledge of the subject recognised that he was affected by the disorder known as megalomania.

As most of Europe's royal families of the era were related, personal contact between their members played a large part in diplomatic activity. Unfortunately, while commenting that war between Germany and Great Britain was 'a most unimaginable thing,' Wilhelm harboured a strong dislike for his English uncle, King Edward VII, stemming from jealousy. Edward did indeed possess an empire on which the sun never set. Wilhelm declared that Germany, too, had a right to 'a place in the sun,' but few of the colonies he began establishing in distant parts of the globe produced an adequate return for their upkeep. Again, Edward's Royal Navy was the largest and most prestigious in the world. Wilhelm admired it and was desperate for a large fleet of his own, the acquisition of which would mean that the German Empire, created as recently as 1870, had indeed become a world power.

In this he was actively encouraged by Admiral Alfred von Tirpitz, who sported the kind of forked beard favoured by pantomime demons. When he became virtual head of the Imperial German Navy in 1897, Tirpitz encouraged Wilhelm's government to spend vast sums on building a battle fleet that would pose a threat to the Royal Navy's dominance, arguing that the risk posed by a rival presence in the North Sea would discourage the British from interfering in Germany's perceived interests around the world.

British naval policy was already to maintain a navy equal in size to the combined naval strength of any two major powers. Tirpitz reasoned, therefore, that in any possible conflict between the British and German navies, the former would sustain losses that would destroy that ratio, even if the Royal Navy was victorious locally. This so-called 'risk theory' was wishful thinking at its worst, as British diplomacy quickly reached an amicable understanding with the United Kingdom's most likely maritime opponents, France and Russia. The immediate result of Tirpitz's avowed intentions was to sour Anglo-German relations and provoke a naval construction race between the two countries. Tirpitz immediately found himself to be at a major disadvantage as the Imperial Army had a prior claim on funds and resources. His construction programme was already lagging when, in 1906, HMS *Dreadnought*, armed with ten 12-inch guns, entered service with the Royal Navy, making every other battleship in the world obsolete. Tirpitz was forced to start from scratch again, not only in the field of designing dreadnought-type battleships, but also in building docks to handle them and widening the Kiel Canal, which was the Imperial Navy's strategic means of passage between the North and Baltic Seas. To make matters worse, in 1908 the Royal Navy introduced an altogether new class of warship, the battle cruiser, which combined the hitting power of the battleship with the speed of the cruiser. As we shall see, there was an inherent flaw in the concept, but for the moment it rendered the heavy cruiser obsolete as a class and set the German designers yet another problem to be solved at short notice. As if this was not bad enough, in 1912 the Royal Navy began arming its latest class of dreadnought with 15-inch guns while the Germans had not progressed beyond a 12-inch main armament for theirs.

By August 1914 the Royal Navy had 20 dreadnought battleships in commission, plus two due for completion by the end of the year, three due for delivery in 1915 and six more in 1916. In addition, three dreadnoughts being built for foreign navies were promptly requisitioned. Nine battle cruisers were already operational and a tenth was serving in the Royal Australian Navy. In contrast, only 15 German dreadnoughts had been commissioned by August 1914, with two more expected in 1915 and another two in 1916. Six battle cruisers were in service, with a seventh due in 1915 and an eighth in 1916.

Tirpitz had annoyed a great many people with his anti-British attitude and incessant demands, but now, thoroughly alarmed, he began agitating for peace. Unfortunately, because of greatly improved relations between Great Britain and France, Germany's historic enemy, there was now a ground-swell of anti-British feeling throughout central Europe. Even if his warnings had been heeded, events were rapidly spiralling out of control. On 28th June 1914 the Austro-Hungarian Archduke Franz Ferdinand and his wife were murdered by a Serbian nationalist in Sarajevo, then part of the Austro-Hungarian Empire. There was a horrible inevitability about the sequence of event that followed. Austria-Hungary threatened to invade Serbia unless the Serbs agreed to accept a series of impossibly humiliating demands. Serbia's protector was Russia, who promised to come to her aid if she was attacked. The contents of this witches' cauldron were already close to bubbling over when Wilhelm, whose forays into international relations were the despair of his diplomatic service, chose to toss in one of his hopelessly ill-considered comments: 'The day of Austro-Hungarian mobilisation, for whatever cause, will be the day of German mobilisation, too!' Then he went on holiday. Encouraged, the Austrians set their war machine in motion. Russia had no alternative but to respond by mobilising her huge army. By the time Wilhelm returned from his jaunt the situation was beyond control. France mobilised in compliance with her understanding with Russia, followed by the United Kingdom, which had similar understandings with both as well as a treaty obligation to protect Belgium, passage through which formed part of the German General

Staff's plan of campaign against France. All the major powers of Europe now found themselves embarked on a full-scale war, little understanding that modern weapons were capable of inflicting slaughter on a truly industrial scale.

The Imperial German Navy might have been one of the Kaiser's favourite toys, but the question of what to do with it now that Great Britain and Germany were actually at war was never satisfactorily resolved. In global terms, a number of German cruisers and gunboats were showing the flag around the world. No one expected them to survive for long and they didn't, but that is another story. Most of the Imperial Navy, was optimistically named the High Seas Fleet, despite being confined to home waters from which it could only be deployed against Russia in the Baltic or the United Kingdom across the North Sea. Admiral Friedrich von Ingenohl, Commander-in-Chief of the High Seas Fleet, immediately dismissed the idea of a major action between his surface ships and the much larger British Grand Fleet as the outcome was entirely predictable. On the other hand, what was to be done with the surface warships on which so much treasure had been lavished and which required tens of thousands of men to man, men whom the Army would gladly have absorbed to replace the horrendous losses of the war's early battles? In the view of Ingenohl, an innately cautious man, the answer was nothing, beyond mine-laying off the English coast, sinking a few British trawlers, regular defensive patrolling in the Heligoland Bight, and gunfire support for the ground troops fighting against the Russians on the Baltic coast. Again, the Kaiser himself insisted that the High Seas Fleet must be preserved as a bargaining counter in the peace talks that would follow shortly after his armies' rapid destruction of their opponents. That, too, proved to be wishful thinking and in a matter of weeks Ingenohl would be forced to commit his ships to battle.

CHAPTER 3

Kicking in the Front Door – The Battle of Heligoland Bight

During the first hour of 26 August 1914 the German cruiser *Magdeburg* ran aground in fog 500 yards off the Odensholm lighthouse in the Baltic. All efforts to refloat the vessel failed and her forecastle was blown off to prevent her falling into enemy hands. Some of the crew were taken off by an accompanying destroyer, but the captain and 56 of his men were taken prisoner when two Russian cruisers arrived on the scene and opened fire, causing the destroyer to beat a hasty retreat. To the Russians' astonishment and delight, the *Magdeburg*'s signal code book, cipher tables and a marked grid chart of the North Sea were recovered from the body of a drowned signalman. They were promptly passed to the British Admiralty which set up a radio intercept intelligence branch known as Room 40. By mid-December the code breakers were able to listen to the Imperial Navy's radio traffic to their hearts' content.

As if this was not bad enough, on 28 August a strong raiding force commanded by Commodore Roger Keyes

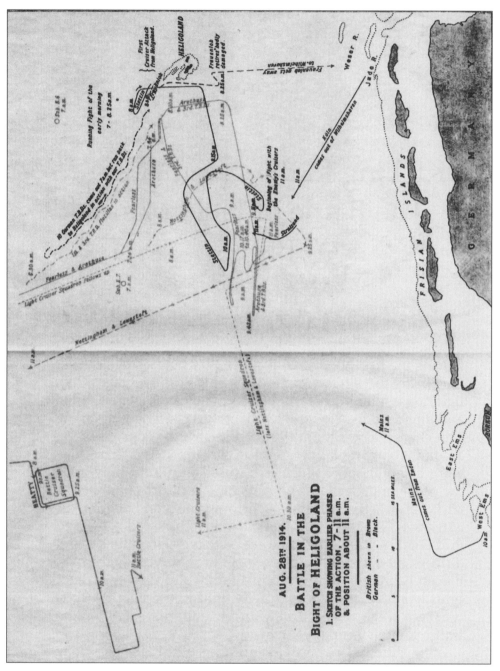

Map 2. The earlier phases of the Battle of Heligoland Bight. 7 to 11am.

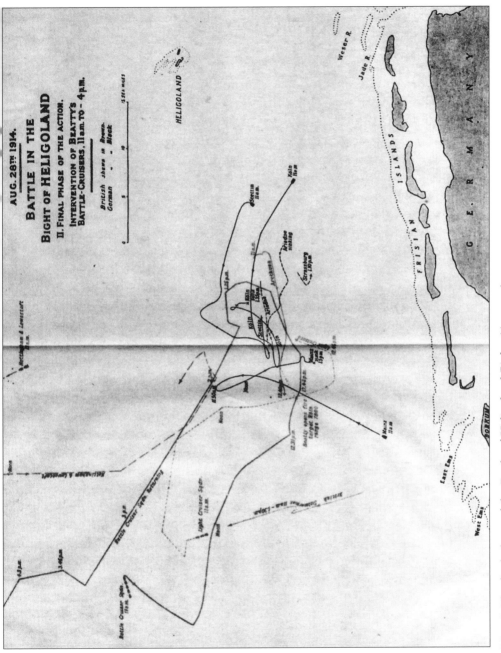

Map 3. The final phase of the Battle of Heligoland Bight. 11am to 4 pm.

penetrated the Heligoland Bight. The raiders were not merely on Germany's doorstep – they were halfway through her front door. In the lead were two destroyer flotillas commanded by Commodore R.Y. Tyrwhitt, followed by the 1st Light Cruiser Squadron under Commodore W.R. Goodenough and Rear Admiral A.H. Christian's 7th Cruiser Squadron. Standing off and ready to intervene or administer the decisive *coup de grace* was Vice Admiral Sir David Beatty's 1st Battle Cruiser Squadron, consisting of the battle cruisers *Lion*, *Princess Royal*, *Queen Mary*, *New Zealand* and *Invincible* with their escorting destroyers. A flotilla of submarines was also attached to the force with the task of alarming the enemy and confusing his response.

The subsequent engagement took place in a flat calm but was a confused affair in which visibility was limited to two or three miles, effectively denying the German coastal defence batteries on Heligoland Island the chance to join in. The British destroyers fought a fast-moving action, sinking one of their opposite numbers, *V-187*. However, at about 08:00, Tyrwhitt's flagship, the light cruiser *Arethusa*, was engaged with a German cruiser, the *Stettin*. Unfortunately, the *Arethusa* had only been commissioned two days previously, so her crew had neither the benefits of a shakedown cruise nor gunnery practice – and, like the ship herself, her guns were also brand new and still prone to jamming. A second enemy cruiser, the *Frauenlob*, joined in the fight and *Arethusa* began to take a battering. Before long all her guns except for the forecastle 6-inch were out of action for various reasons, an ammunition fire had broken out and casualties were rising. Luckily, at this point the light cruiser *Fearless*, the leader of the 1st Destroyer Flotilla, arrived and drew off *Stettin*'s fire. At 08:25 one of *Arethusa*'s shells exploded on *Frauenlob*'s forebridge, killing everyone in the bridge party, including her captain. She sheered away out of the battle in the direction of Heligoland, covered by *Stettin*. The first phase of the battle was over.

The High Seas Fleet command, believing that the only enemy ships in the area were *Arethusa*, *Fearless* and the destroyers, now began directing more of its own cruisers into the Bight. Fighting was renewed at about 10:00, by which time *Arethusa* had recovered the use of all but two of her guns although her maximum speed had been reduced to ten knots. Having seen *Frauenlob* safely out of the action, *Stettin* returned to the fray, followed by *Stralsund*, which immediately became involved in a duel with *Arethusa*. Four more German cruisers, *Koln*, *Kolberg*, *Strassburg* and *Ariadne*, entered the fight shortly after so that by 11:00 Tyrwhitt found himself in the midst of a thoroughly disturbed hornet's nest. He sent a radio signal to Beatty, still some distance away to the north-west, requesting urgent assistance. Beatty despatched Commodore Goodenough's light cruiser squadron immediately and followed with his battle cruisers at about 11:30.

For those British cruisers and destroyers already engaged with the enemy, there was the constant fear that the German battle cruisers would emerge from their anchorage in the Jade River and send them to the bottom before help could arrive. They need not have worried, for in the present state of the tide the enemy's heavy warships drew too much water for them to be able to cross the sandbar at the river's mouth, a situation that would not change until the afternoon. In the meantime, senior German commanders could only fume with rage and frustration while the battle took its course.

Goodenough's light cruisers arrived at about noon. When, at 12:15, the battle cruisers, led by Beatty in *Lion*, burst out of the northern mist, there could no longer be any doubt as to the battle's outcome.

Three of the enemy's light cruisers, *Mainz*, *Koln* and *Ariadne*, were sunk after fighting to the bitter end, and the rest escaped in a damaged condition. In addition, the battle cost Germany 1,200 officers and men killed or captured. Among those killed aboard the *Koln* was Rear Admiral

21

Leberecht Maas, commander of the German light forces in the Bight. The British destroyer *Lurcher* rescued many survivors from the *Mainz*, including Lieutenant von Tirpitz, son of the German Minister of Marine. Winston Churchill, then First Lord of the Admiralty, chivalrously arranged for the International Red Cross to advise the Admiral that the young officer had survived the battle. British casualties amounted to 35 killed and some 40 wounded. Most of the damage sustained was repaired in a week.

The outcome of the battle created a tremendous sense of shock throughout Germany. The Kaiser sent for his Chief of Naval Staff, Admiral Hugo von Pohl. He was horrified by the loss that had been incurred during a comparatively minor engagement and impressed upon Pohl that the fleet should refrain from fighting 'actions that can lead to greater losses.' Pohl promptly telegraphed Ingenohl to the effect that 'In his anxiety to preserve the fleet His Majesty requires you to wire for his consent before entering a decisive action.' In other words, before involving the High Seas Fleet in any sort of large scale action, Ingenohl, a professional naval officer of many years standing, should seek the advice of that old sea dog, Wilhelm Hohenzollern.

The battle and its aftermath marked the beginning of the end of Tirpitz's career. The admiral had produced a fleet of fine ships that were in some respects better than those of the Royal Navy. They were, for example, compartmentalised to a greater extent, enabling them to withstand considerable punishment, and they were equipped with fine optical gunsights. Understandably, he did not wish to see his creation destroyed in a fleet action, but neither did he want to see it tied up at its moorings for the duration of the war. In his memoirs, written in 1919, he expressed outrage at Wilhelm's diktat:

Order issued by the Emperor following an audience with Pohl – to which I was not summoned – restricted the initiative of the Commander-in-Chief North Sea

Fleet. The loss of ships was to be avoided, while fleet sallies and any greater undertakings must be approved by His Majesty in advance. I took the first opportunity to explain to the Emperor the fundamental error of such a muzzling policy.

This argument met with no success; on the contrary, there sprang up from that day forth an estrangement between the Emperor and myself which steadily increased.

Today, Pohl's name means nothing to most people, even in Germany, yet there were two remarkable things about him. First, in 1913 he had been honoured in Great Britain by an appointment as a Companion of the Order of the Bath, a surprising adornment for one of the most senior officers in a rival navy. Secondly, he was quick to realise that the Imperial Navy's U-boat arm was capable of inflicting far greater damage on the enemy than the surface fleet. Although the German light cruiser *Hela* was torpedoed and sunk by the British submarine *E-9* (commanded by the then Lieutenant Max Horton, who became Commander-in-Chief Western Approaches during World War Two) the months of September and October 1914 belonged to the U-boats, which fully justified Pohl's opinion of their potential. On 5 September the light cruiser *Pathfinder* was torpedoed off the Scottish coast and sank with heavy loss of life. On 22 September Lieutenant Otto Weddigen's *U-9* sank, in turn, the elderly cruiser *Aboukir*, then her sister ship *Hogue* as she was picking up survivors, then a third sister, *Cressey*, which opened an ineffective fire against the submarine's periscope. Of the 1,459 officers and men manning the three cruisers, many of them elderly reservists, only 779 were rescued by nearby trawlers. Weddigen's remarkable feat earned him Imperial Germany's most coveted award, the *Pour le Merite*. On 15 October *U-9* claimed a further victim in the North Sea, the ancient protected cruiser *Hawke* which, having been launched in 1893, had really reached the end of her useful life. The same month saw the seaplane carrier *Hermes* torpedoed and sunk by *U-27*. In addition, U-boats had sunk a modest tonnage of Allied merchant shipping, although this would rise to horrific levels as the war progressed. To end a very depressing month, the dreadnought battleship *Audacious* struck a mine laid by the armed merchant cruiser *Berlin* off the north coast of Ireland and sank as the result of an internal explosion.

CHAPTER 4

Off to Yarmouth for the Day

By the end of October Admiral Ingenohl was on the horns of a dilemma. The U-boat sinkings made excellent reading for the German public, but the High Seas Fleet had achieved very little and its morale was deteriorating as it swung idly around its anchors in obedience to the Kaiser's diktat. What made the position even more difficult was the fact that those isolated German naval units still at sea were, so far, giving a good account of themselves. Off East Africa, for instance, the light cruiser *Konigsberg* had engaged and sunk the elderly British cruiser *Pegasus* in Zanzibar harbour. It had not been much of a fight as *Pegasus* was engaged in cleaning her boilers and was therefore nothing more than a stationary hulk whose guns were outranged by 1,000 yards. For the moment, *Konigsberg* had vanished as completely as if she had never existed.

In the Far East another light cruiser, the *Emden*, commanded by Captain Karl von Müller, had sunk the Russian cruiser *Yemtschuk* (sometimes spelled *Zemchug*) and the French destroyer *Mousquet* in Penang harbour. Müller had then gone on a rampage around the Indian Ocean, sinking 21 Allied merchant ships, destroying cargo valued at £3 million and even bombarding Madras. The *Emden* was still at large and was being hunted as a matter of urgency by the British and Australian navies. At large in the Pacific was Vice Admiral Maximilian Graf von Spee's East Asiatic Squadron, consisting of the armoured cruisers *Scharnhorst* and *Gneisenau* and several light cruisers. In time of peace, the squadron was based at Tsingtao, which was then a German treaty port and naval base on the coast of China. It was now believed to be replenishing its coal somewhere off the west coast of South America prior to rounding Cape Horn and entering the Atlantic.

In the circumstances, therefore, it was incumbent upon Ingenohl to devise one or more operations that would avoid placing the High Seas Fleet in danger yet have a profound effect on British and German public opinion. These would involve raids on England's east coast towns using the fleet's fast battle cruisers, cruisers and minlayers. The British Grand Fleet was not large enough to protect the entire coastline and many areas were covered by elderly or light naval units. Nevertheless, the Grand Fleet would have to react to such a raid and if part of it could be ambushed and destroyed, this would bring the respective strengths of the two fleets closer together. In time, Ingenohl hoped, sufficient parity would be achieved for the High Seas Fleet to win a significant victory. Moreover, even if major elements of the Grand Fleet could not be lured into an ambush after specific raids, the fact was that the High Seas Fleet was able to carry out such raids at all was proof that Britannia no longer ruled the waves and that the Royal Navy was incapable of doing its job. This aspect as much as any other appealed to the Kaiser, who gave Ingernohl permission to proceed.

The first objective was the seaside resort and port of Great Yarmouth on the Norfolk coast. More commonly known simply as Yarmouth, the harbour also provided limited naval facilities. Commanding the raiding force was Vice Admiral Franz Hipper, a Bavarian who had been appointed commander of the High Seas Fleet's Scouting Forces. On this occasion his force included the battle cruisers *Seydlitz*,

Von der Tann and *Moltke*, the armoured cruiser *Blücher* and the four light cruisers *Strassburg*, *Graudenz*, *Kolberg* and *Stralsund*, the last with 100 mines aboard.

The raiding force left the Jade River at 16:30 on 2 November, followed later by two battleship squadrons whose task was to ambush any British warships that were pursuing the battle cruisers on their return journey. At 06:30 the following morning the raiders swept past a buoy which was identified as the Smith's Knoll marker and were able to confirm their precise position. As they closed in on Yarmouth, a flashing light challenged two of the German cruisers. They immediately opened fire on its source, the minesweeper *Halcyon*, which was soon surrounded by fountains of water thrown up by bursting German shells of all calibres, although the damage inflicted was slight and only three of her crew were injured. On this occasion German gunnery was extremely poor due to inefficient fire discipline. Instead of allowing one ship to fire ranging salvos, all the battle cruisers blazed away at once so that none of them were able to identify their own splashes. Consequently, they were unable to adjust their range settings with any degree of accuracy. At this point two British destroyers, *Lively* and *Leopard*, entered the scene, causing further confusion when *Lively* began to make smoke that concealed the target behind an oily black fog. At 07:40 Hipper ordered the battle cruisers to shift their fire from *Lively* to Yarmouth itself. The result resembled nothing so much as pure *opera bouffe* for, once again, gunnery officers failed to provide their gun crews with an accurate range. Explosions erupted along the shoreline and tons of sand were blown skywards, but little or no damage was done.

Stralsund now signalled Hipper that she had completed laying her mines in the area of Smith's Knoll and the admiral gave the order for the raiding force to withdraw, which it did at speed. In the meantime *Halcyon* despatched a radio signal reporting the presence of the raiders. A third destroyer, *Success*, joined *Lively* and *Leopard*, while three more raised steam inside the harbour. Simultaneously, three submarines, *E-10*, *D-3* and *D-5*, glided past the mole and out into the open sea in the hope of sinking one at least of Hipper's ships. In was a vain hope, for the latter were now running for home at full speed. During the pursuit, *D-5* struck one of *Stralsund*'s mines and sank, taking 21 of her crew with her.

Despite *Halcyon*'s warning, it was 09:55 before Admiral Beatty's battle cruisers were ordered south from their Scottish anchorage, followed by the Grand Fleet's battle squadrons. Part of the reason for the delay was that news had just been received that on 1 November an action had taken place between the German East Asia Squadron and a much smaller British squadron under Rear Admiral Sir Christopher Cradock off Coronel on the west coast of South America. Two old cruisers, *Monmouth* and *Good Hope*, had been sunk with all hands. The reasons for the defeat were simple. Slow, under-gunned ships could not hope to get within range of faster, more powerfully armed opponents. The latter would dictate the range at which the battle would be fought, and as the former could neither fight nor flee, their end was inevitable. Cradock was dead but his squadron's survivors, the light cruiser *Glasgow* and the armed merchant cruiser *Otranto*, had made good their escape, as he had ordered them to. He was, however, criticised for discarding a fifth warship prior to the action. This was the pre-dreadnought battleship *Canopus* with a main armament of four 12-inch guns but a maximum speed of only 12 knots, well below that of any of Spee's ships. At first Admiral Sir John Jellicoe, commanding the Grand Fleet, could not be contacted because he was aboard a train, but as soon as he was advised of the situation he sanctioned the despatch of two battle cruisers, *Invincible* and *Inflexible*, to the South Atlantic under the command of Vice Admiral Sir Doveton Sturdee. The fact that the Royal Navy had actually lost a battle created a sense of shock that completely eclipsed what had taken place off Yarmouth. However, from his perspective as First Lord of the Admiralty, Winston Churchill was unable to see anything more in the German attack than a badly executed raid.

By the time Beatty's battle cruisers were at sea, Hipper's ships were 50 miles from Yarmouth and well on their way home, but thanks to a dense fog both they and the ambush force were unable to enter harbour that night and were forced to heave to in the approach area known as Schillig Roads. This resulted in the most serious loss of the entire operation. Aboard the armoured cruiser *Yorck*, part of the ambush force, typhus was believed to be present in the ship's drinking water tanks and her commander, a Captain Peiper, requested leave to return to port. He was given permission to do so, subject to visibility improving. He subsequently denied receiving the condition attached to the approval. The result was that on the way into Wilhelmshaven, *Yorck* was steered past the wrong side of a buoy and into a defensive minefield in which she struck two mines, then capsized and sank. Fortunately, she went down in shallow water, permitting the rescue of 381 survivors sitting on the up-turned hull, but a further 336 men were drowned. It was a poor exchange for one small British submarine that was approaching obsolescence. Peiper survived but could not be described as a lucky captain as the previous year he had been dismissed from the *Blücher* for running her aground. Following his court martial for losing the *Yorck* he was sent to manage a munitions factory in Turkey, an appointment that must have raised a number of eyebrows.

Naturally, the Kaiser was delighted with the result of the Battle of Coronel, but the fact that the High Seas Fleet had actually carried out a raid into British home waters, despite its dubious results, almost certainly gave Wilhelm equal pleasure, for he awarded Hipper the Iron Cross. Hipper, well aware that far more was required to merit the decoration than blowing holes in someone's holiday beach, declined to wear it as he had no wish to be regarded as a laughing stock.

CHAPTER 5

Admiral Ingenohl Decides to Go Home

Even when formal operations were not taking place, some sort of warlike activity, often clandestine, was always happening in the North Sea. In October 1914 the minelayer *Berlin* managed to avoid the patrols of the Royal Navy's northern blockade by passing between Iceland and the Faroes. She then laid the minefield off the northern Irish coast that had accounted for the battleship *Audacious* and, having negotiated the Denmark Strait, reached Trondheim in Norway, where she was interned.

On 17 October the 3rd Destroyer Flotilla, consisting of the light cruiser *Undaunted* and the destroyers *Lance*, *Lennox*, *Legion* and *Loyal*, was patrolling an area known as the Broad Fourteens, about 40 miles south-west of the Texel, when it encountered four small German destroyers, *S-115*, *S-117*, *S-118* and *S-119*, similarly engaged. Despite being heavily outgunned the Germans, all armed with three 1.9-inch guns while *Undaunted* mounted two 6-inch and six 4-inch guns and the four British destroyer three 4-inch guns apiece, put up a what has been described as a spirited fight before they were all sent to the bottom.

Meanwhile, the light cruiser *Karlsruhe* had been creating mayhem in the West Indies, where she had sunk 70,000 tons of British shipping. Her career had come to a dramatic end when, some 200 miles off Trinidad, she sustained fatal damage and sank as a result of a major internal explosion for which there was no immediate explanation. During the period of coal firing, a number of ships had been lost because of explosions in their coal bunkers caused by the dangerous combination of coal dust and air, and this may have been *Karlsruhe*'s fate. Her supply ship *Rio Negro* picked up her survivors and also managed to evade the British blockade and reach Norway in November.

In the major sphere of events, Admiral Ingenohl was so encouraged by the apparent success of the raid on Great Yarmouth that he pressed for greater activity by the High Seas Fleet in the North Sea itself, especially as the margin by which the Germans were outnumbered had been reduced by the despatch of two of the Grand Fleet's battle cruisers to deal with von Spee's East Asiatic Squadron. With the exception of the light cruiser *Dresden*, which had made good her escape, Spee's command had been destroyed in a battle fought on 8 December south of the Falkland Islands. Aware that the two British battle cruisers were already on their way home, Ingenohl planned a second raid on eastern England at short notice, choosing multiple targets for greater effect.

He decided that the strike would take place along the North Yorkshire coast. The area selected lay between known naval bases on the Tyne and the Humber and access to it was possible through minefields laid off the coast by the Germans themselves, by means of a gap opposite Scarborough and Whitby. Further advantages were that the British naval presence in the immediate target area consisted of elderly or obsolete light forces, and that it lay due west of the German naval bases in the Elbe and Jade rivers. A major disadvantage was that it was much closer to the Grand Fleet's Scottish anchorages than Yarmouth and a real danger existed that the raiding force might be caught before it reached home. For this reason Ingenohl decided to support Hipper's battle cruisers with the major part of the High Seas Fleet, which would intervene if Hipper was attacked and, hopefully, inflict serious loss on the enemy.

The specific targets were the ports of Hartlepool, Whitby and Scarborough. Hartlepool was a busy, bustling place that over the years had become a conurbation including West Hartlepool. Its harbour possessed two major basins. Businesses included shipbuilding, engineering and the hand-ling of general cargo including the export of coal and the import of millions of pit props every year from Scandinavia. Its defences included two permanent coastal defence batteries, the Heugh (pronounced Huff) Battery with two guns and the Lighthouse Battery with one gun, armament in each case consisting of 6-inch Mark VII guns with a maximum range of 11,800 yards. Some four miles to the south the South Gare Battery at Teesmouth was armed with two 4.7-inch guns with a maximum range of 15,500 yards, and a third 4.7-inch was being mounted on the Old Pier. All batteries were manned by the Territorial gunners of the Durham Royal Garrison Artillery with close defence provided by the 18th Durham Light Infantry, a Pals battalion raised shortly after the outbreak of war.

In addition to the coastal defence artillery, a number of small warships were based in the harbour. These included four E (River) Class destroyers (*Doon*, *Moy*, *Waveney* and *Test*) which possessed a fair turn of speed at 26 knots and were armed with four 12-pdr guns and two 18-inch torpedo tubes apiece. With the River Class of 1904, destroyers had become sea-going ships capable of escorting the fleet at sea. At Hartlepool they carried out daily patrols offshore with the support of two larger warships officially classed as Scouts, *Patrol* and *Forward*. These had entered service in 1905 and were designed as light, fast cruisers specifically designed to work with the River Class destroyers. They were capable of 25 knots and armed with nine 4-inch guns and two 14-inch torpedo tubes. Also present in the harbour was the tiny C Class coastal submarine *C-7*. When surfaced the boat was capable of 14 knots and driven by a petrol engine that made an already dangerous profession even more hazardous; submerged, the boat's electric motors could produce a maximum speed of 10 knots. With a complement of sixteen, *C-7* possessed two 18-inch torpedo tubes in the bow but could only employ these when surfaced, which destroyed the element of concealment necessary in submarine warfare.

It can therefore be seen that Hartlepool was making a very considerable contribution to the national war effort. This consideration did not apply to quite the same extent at Whitby, which was primarily a fishing port situated in a long, steep-sided valley, although it did possess a number of claims to fame. Even today, most people have heard of the Synod of Whitby, if not that it was an assembly of learned divines who met in AD 664 to decide how to crack the problem of calculating the date of Easter. Then there was Captain James Cook, the renowned navigator and hydrographer who was born not far away and completed his apprenticeship aboard a Whitby collier carrying coal to London before enlisting in the Royal Navy. More recently, Count Dracula, the novelist Bram Stoker's unpleasant brain child, had attracted the curious to the town by coming ashore at Whitby, having travelled by ship from Romania inside a comfortable coffin. Of more practical interest were nearby deposits of alum, used in tanning and dyeing, and good quality jet that could be expertly carved into mourning jewellery. However, the only military installation in the area was a coastguard signal station on the sea cliffs above the town, and that scarcely merited a special visit from Hipper's battle cruiser force.

The same could be said of Scarborough, an elegant and rather stylish resort some miles to the south. In this respect German intelligence was hopelessly at fault. In German eyes, Scarborough, was a 'fortress town,' although the only 'fortress' was a ruined medieval castle on the headland separating the resort's North and South Bays. It had undergone a protracted siege during the English Civil War, after which it had been thoroughly slighted to prevent its ever being defended again. During the Napoleonic Wars Scarborough's coast defences had consisted of 15 guns, some at least of which had been mounted on the headland, but in 1914 the only gun present was a trophy captured from the Russians during the Crimean War, almost sixty years earlier. Yet, when the German Navy's official history of the war was written, with appropriate access being granted to British records to its authors, it was claimed that 'at Scarborough it was known that during peacetime there was a battery of six 6-inch quick-firing guns and three other guns of this calibre that were not mounted.' Perhaps this was included as an attempt to save face in view of what actually happened, but the majority of Germans sincerely believed that the town was defended. During the 1950s I encountered a former German seaman who had taken part in the raid and he, along with the rest of the crew, had been assured by his captain that this was the case. In fact, although a small barracks existed, it was home to a few Yeomanry troopers, who exercised their horses on the shore, and a handful of infantrymen. Otherwise, the only legitimate targets available were the coastguard station, the lighthouse, the gasworks and a wireless station behind the town.

The force which Hipper would employ against this motley selection of targets included his 1st and 2nd Scouting Groups. The former consisted of the battle cruisers *Seydlitz*, *Moltke*, *Von der Tann* and *Derfflinger*, plus the heavy cruiser *Blücher*. *Seydlitz* and *Moltke* which were armed with ten 11-inch guns, twelve 5.9-inch guns and twelve 3.4-inch guns; *Von der Tann* was the first German battle cruiser to have been completed and, being somewhat smaller than her successors, was armed with eight 11-inch guns, ten 5.9-inch guns and sixteen 3.4-inch guns; *Derfflinger*, the most recently commissioned, was also the most heavily armed with eight 12-inch guns, twelve 5.9-inch guns and eight 3.4-inch guns. *Blücher* was something of a hybrid. Originally conceived as a battle cruiser, her designers had been deceived into believing that the main armament calibre of the British Invincible Class battle cruisers would be 8.2-inches. By the time it was discovered that the Invincibles mounted 12-inch guns it was too late. *Blücher* was down-graded to the status of armoured cruiser, but as she carried reasonable protection and was capable of 26 knots, just one knot slower than the German battle cruisers, she was attached to the 1st Scouting Group. In any event, the plan was to use only the ships' secondary and tertiary armaments against the British shore targets and save the larger calibre shells for use against a major enemy naval vessel, should the chance arise.

Following prior reconnaissance by *U-27* under Lieutenant Commander Wegener, Hipper's force put to sea at 02:00 (times quoted are British unless otherwise stated) on 15 December, heading for a point 170 nautical miles north-north-west of Heligoland at a common speed of 15 knots. With the light starting to fade, at 14:30 the German destroyers and the four light cruisers of the 2nd Scouting Group formed a screen four miles ahead and to port and starboard of the battle cruisers. Until now, visibility had been good and the wind light, but at about 18:00 the wind freshened, bringing with it a rainsquall, and a steady deterioration in the weather followed. At about the same time course was altered to west-south-west by west, which would take Hipper's force past the northern edge of Dogger Bank on a heading for the target area.

Meanwhile, between 16:00 and 21:00 the High Seas Fleet's I, II, III and IV Battle Squadrons had put to sea and assembled 20 nautical miles north of Heligoland. In total, Ingenohl had 14 dreadnoughts and eight older battleships at his disposal, plus escorting cruisers and destroyers, which he led on a west-south-westerly course towards the eastern edge of Dogger Bank, from which he could cover Hipper's withdrawal once the bombardments had taken place. Far away to the west, *Moltke*'s radio operators were monitoring the British frequencies. Between 19:00 and 20:30 the traffic on these decreased and finally tailed off altogether. The conclusion drawn was that British submarines in the Heligoland Bight were reporting the emergence of the High Seas Fleet.

If Ingenohl and Hipper had known the truth they would have been horrified. The naval codes taken from the wreck of the *Magdeburg* by the Russians and passed to the British Admiralty had just been broken and Room 40 of Naval Intelligence was fully aware that Hipper's battle cruisers had embarked on another raid, though not of Ingenohl's presence. Early on the morning of 15 December Vice Admiral Sir David Beatty was despatched south from Cromarty with his four available battle cruisers: *Lion*, *Princess Royal*, *Queen Mary* and *New Zealand*. Simultaneously, Vice Admiral Sir George Warrender's 2nd Battle Squadron, consisting of the dreadnought battleships *King George V*, *Ajax*, *Centurion*, *Orion*, *Monarch* and *Conqueror* was ordered down from Scapa Flow at full speed. This was easier said than done, for outside the Flow the weather conditions were atrocious and the seas so heavy that two attached cruisers, *Blanche* and *Boadicea*, were forced to return to the anchorage. *Boadicea*, in fact, had her bridge washed away and several of her crew were swept overboard without any prospect of rescue. The destroyers were unable to get out of the Flow at all, but seven of those based at Cromarty were ordered to put to sea and join Beatty, which they succeeded in doing. Warrender caught up with Beatty at about noon and three hours later was reinforced by the 3rd Cruiser Squadron, consisting of the heavy cruisers *Antrim*, *Devonshire*, *Argyll* and *Roxburgh*. As the combined force ploughed southwards parallel to the Scottish coast in the gathering darkness with the destroyers covering the eastern flank, the weather eased a little although the night remained exceptionally dark. Beatty was steering towards a point south of Dogger Bank, little suspecting that this was just 30 nautical miles beyond the rendezvous area in which the High Seas Fleet was to await Hipper's return from the English coast. In fact, at about 01:00 Hipper crossed Beatty's intended course some 10 to 15 miles ahead of the British battle cruisers.

Some form of contact between Beatty and the High Seas Fleet was now inevitable. It was provided by a Lieutenant Buddecke, the acting commander of the destroyer *S-33*, which formed part of Hipper's screen. The destroyers forming the advance screen had difficulty in maintaining their correct station ahead of the battle cruisers and had been told to maintain contact with *S-33*, which seems to have been located in an intermediate position between the forward screen and *Seydlitz*, the flagship. At about 02:00 Buddecke lost contact with everyone. Overwhelmed with the responsibility he panicked and, contrary to strict instructions, broke radio silence on four occasions between 02:14 and 02:43 in an attempt to contact the screen commander aboard the cruiser *Strassburg*. Declining to respond, *Strassburg* jammed his signal. Buddecke did not know the location of the High Seas Fleet's rendezvous area and, feeling rather lonely by now, he set course for the island of Sylt. Suddenly, at about 06:00, the shapes of four destroyers in line ahead appeared only 150 yards distant, steering south at slow speed. What Buddecke did next almost certainly saved him from the court martial he had undoubtedly earned. Recognising that the destroyers could only be British, he swung on to a parallel course and reduced his speed to conform to theirs. As there was no reaction he slowly turned away to the east and by 06:20 had broken contact altogether. An hour later he observed the flashes of gunfire away to the west but avoided his earlier misdemeanour by not reporting his encounter until 10:55.

The gunfire resulted from an engagement between the German destroyer *V-155*, commanded by Lieutenant Carl, which formed part of the High Seas Fleet's advance screen and, having been detached by the screen commander to investigate a steamer, had run into Beatty's destroyers. Carl's report on the action was imaginative, to say the least. Having reported the enemy's presence by radio, as he was entitled to do by virtue of the fact that he was already in action with them, he comments that he was chased away to the north by no less than 12 and possibly as many as 16 destroyers, an estimate corrected to seven by the German official historian after the war. The chase was abandoned at about 08:38, by which time it was becoming light, enabling Carl to rejoin the screen forty minutes later. Despite the heroics, he had done well against the odds, scoring hits on the *Lynx* and the *Ambuscade*.

That, however, was not quite the end of the matter. On receiving Carl's radio report, the light cruiser *Hamburg* under Lieutenant Commander von Gaudecker, and two destroyers, *V-158* and *V-160*, promptly headed towards the gunfire flashes to assist Carl. Fifteen minutes later *Hamburg*'s searchlight illuminated a destroyer that failed to answer the flashed recognition signal. The destroyer turned as though to release a torpedo at *Hamburg* and Gaudecker took evasive action as well as opening fire. His first salvo went wild but he believed, incorrectly, that his second and subsequent salvos had sunk his opponent. Simultaneously, *Hamburg* was herself hit by two shells, one of which exploded beneath the forward searchlight while the other burst in a wing passage, wrecking a cabin and wounding a gun crew. Gaudecker turned south-east to avoid losing contact with the fleet. His two destroyers conformed, but their fire was masked by *Hamburg* herself and they played little part in the action.

These contacts came as a severe shock to Ingenohl. If British destroyers were involved, he reasoned correctly, they were screening a force that contained much larger warships. Just what was the size of the force opposing him he had no idea, but it might just be the whole Grand Fleet. The truth was that the relative strengths of the two fleets was everything that the German planners had hoped and prayed for. One can only speculate on what might have happened if an engagement had been fought. Beatty was a fighter. He commanded a gunboat during Kitchener's Nile campaign against the dervishes and he had seen yet more fighting in China during the Boxer Rising, but in the present circumstances he had no idea that he had almost run into the High Seas Fleet. If he had attacked he would have been dangerously out-numbered and probably lost ships in a general engagement. If he had opted for retreat, the German ships were slower and would have had to abandon a tail chase, but the public reaction to the Royal Navy running away, to say nothing of the international implications, would be horrific. The brawl between the destroyers warned him that something very big was taking place, but he had no idea what. Before he could reach a decision he received two signals. The first came from the *Patrol* at Hartlepool and the Tyne guard ship *Jupiter* to the effect that they were engaged with two German battle cruisers. The second came from the Admiralty and was a report that Scarborough was being bombarded. Beatty now knew what he had to do. He and Warrender must go after Hipper, catch and destroy him.

Ingenohl, too, had reached a decision. At 06:45 he ordered the fleet to bear away to the south-east at maximum speed.

It had to be accepted that our main body (i.e. the High Seas Fleet) had been sighted. As a result of the high speed of our advance, 15 knots, a large (coal) smoke cloud hung over the fleet and was highly visible. Our own screening forces were weak and in contact with modern enemy reconnaissance forces that could not be overcome. It was highly likely that during the next night the English destroyers would attack the German (i.e. Heligoland) Bight and as the night are particularly dark this would probably lead to ship losses.

An advance by day to join with the Commander of the Reconnaissance Force (i.e. Hipper) was without pressing grounds and did not correspond with the orders from the All Highest about the use of the High Seas Fleet.

In other words, everyone was going home except Hipper, who was being left to look after himself. Ingenohl's reference to the All Highest* refers to the Kaiser's specific instructions that his fleet was not to be risked in general actions, but this failed to satisfy many people, including Tirpitz and the Navy's official historian, who pulled the rest of his argument to pieces. Never again would the High Seas Fleet be presented with such a favourable opportunity.

Meanwhile the British destroyers, led by Commander Jones aboard the *Shark*, continued to probe the German screen, which had now become Ingenohl's rearguard. At one point they opened fire on five German destroyers but when the armoured cruiser *Roon* intervened they were forced to turn away. They maintained contact at longer range and attempted, unsuccessfully, to signal details of the enemy's movements to Admiral Warrender. Visibility began to deteriorate, varying between one and four miles. *Roon*, the command ship of the enemy screen, attempted to take advantage of this by leading a counter-attack on her tormentors with three light cruisers, but Jones increased his speed to 30 knots and bore away to the north. Finally, the Germans turned eastwards after their retiring fleet and disappeared from view in the murk.

It had been an interesting night's work. On both sides ships had been damaged but none had been lost and casualties had been minimal. Yet in its way the encounter had been decisive.

---

* All Highest (Altesse) was one of the Kaiser's forms of address. Wry German humour had it that on Sundays the All Highest communed with the All High.

CHAPTER 6

Dawn Bombardment – The German Bombardments of Scarborough, Whitby and Hartlepool

Along the north-east coast of England the afternoon of 15 December 1914 merged into a grey, raw mid-winter dusk. There was an unpleasant sea running, smashing its way into the foot of the cliffs or rolling up the beaches with a roar of breaking surf. In places the horizon vanished behind a haar, a Scottish term that adequately describes a shifting sea mist.

In Scarborough, Whitby and Hartlepool the lamplighters went about their business, pools of yellow gaslight marking their progress along streets. The illuminated windows of houses and the smoking chimneys above hinted at cosy interiors and warm fires within. Businesses closed their offices, shopkeepers put up their shutters and people hurried home for their evening meal through the dark, breath steaming as they wrapped their coats and scarves the tighter round them. Very few visitors stayed in Scarborough at this time of year and the thoughts of hoteliers were concentrated on how best they could fill their empty rooms during the approaching Festive Season. In Whitby it was the opinion of fisher folk that only necessity would drive a man to sea on such a night. In Hartlepool the scenes and sounds were slightly different. Factory workers on night shifts passed those who had just finished work and were heading for home. From West Hartlepool came the sounds of the railway's nightly clank and puffing as the wagons of incoming and outgoing trains were shunted into the correct order.

There was, therefore, nothing to suggest that this evening was different from any that had gone before. There was, however, a difference. At the Heugh and Lighthouse Batteries the gunners and their infantry close defence riflemen had followed their normal practice and stood to at their action stations as the light faded. An hour after sunset they were stood down and went to supper. Some had duties to perform, others cleaned their kit for the following day and others were allowed into town, provided they returned by Lights Out. The infantrymen began their guard duty, pacing the perimeter of the batteries in pairs, two hours on and four off, until they were relieved at the dawn stand to.

The senior officer present, Lieutenant Colonel Lancelot Robson, a local man, left for his headquarters in West Hartlepool's Grand Hotel. Robson was the sort of man that Field Marshal Montgomery would later describe as being 'twice a citizen.' He had taken an active part in local affairs and at one stage had become Hartlepool's mayor, while as a Volunteer and then a Territorial he had given forty years' service to the town's guns, being commissioned in 1890. The impression we have of him is of a good disciplinarian who trained his men well and earned their respect. Now aged 59, Robson was too old for active service in the field and had retired on the outbreak of war, only to be recalled a fortnight later. His present title was Fortress Commander, with responsibility for the two Hartlepool batteries and the South Gare Battery.

Before proceeding further it is necessary to explain that at this period the Royal Regiment of Artillery was sub-divided into the Royal Horse Artillery, the Royal Field Artillery and the Royal Garrison Artillery. The RGA manned the heaviest guns, including the coastal defence artillery. Officers serving in coastal defence batteries were considered to be something of an elite, having developed fire control systems that were capable of engaging and destroying distant moving targets in all sorts of weather conditions.

At about midnight Robson's immediate superior passed on to him a signal received from the Admiralty. It was deliberately vague in its content, urging that a sharp lookout be maintained along the East Coast at dawn on 16 December, but only by responsible officers who were to keep the warning a secret. As Robson's own standing orders required the batteries to stand to with the guns manned an hour before first light, there was nothing more that he could do apart from arranging for transport to collect him in time for this. The instructions given to the senior naval officer present, Commodore George Ballard, were more specific but also lacked an explanation. The four Hartlepool destroyers, *Test*, *Moy*, *Doon* and *Waveney*, under Lieutenant Commander Fraser, were ordered to carry out their usual dawn sweep, despite the worsening weather, while the remaining warships were to be brought to a state of readiness. One can only guess at the language of the destroyer crews as they up-anchored at 05:45 and steamed out past the breakwater into the heaving darkness.

Meanwhile, at sea Admiral Hipper's ships had entered the minefield gap and were having an equally rough time of it. Hipper received a signal from the 2nd Scouting Group to the effect that conditions were so bad that the light cruisers and destroyers would be unable to man their guns. When a problem of this magnitude arose in the German service, it was normal for the General or Admiral involved to assess it with his Chief of Staff and adopt the best solution proposed. In this case Hipper held a lengthy discussion with his own Chief of Staff, Commander Erich Raeder, who would one day become the German Navy's Commander-in-Chief and achieve the rank of Grand Admiral. In the circumstances it was agreed that there was no point in the lighter vessels remaining and they were ordered to make for the point originally chosen by Ingenohl as the High Seas Fleet's rendezvous, a decision reached in ignorance of the fact that the fleet was actually on its way home. The exception to this was the light cruiser *Kolberg*, which was to lay a minefield off Filey, to the south of Scarborough. Hipper, confident that his battle cruisers provided steady enough platforms for accurate gunnery, declined to abort the operation and in the event the decision to detach his smaller warships proved to be a blessing in disguise.

Aboard *Seydlitz* with Hipper, was an officer who had taken part in *U-27*'s earlier reconnaissance of the coastline and was familiar with the various landmarks. Shortly after the dark smudge of the English coast broke the horizon it was possible to pinpoint the force's position precisely. Hipper now divided his group, despatching *Kolberg* south to lay her mines, together with *Von der Tann* and *Derfflinger*, which would bombard Scarborough and Whitby while *Seydlitz*, *Moltke* and *Blücher* swung away to the north with the Hartlepools as their objective.

As the grey dawn strengthened the southern bombardment force, commanded by Rear Admiral Tapken, extinguished its navigation lights and, having obtained an accurate fix as it passed Robin Hood's Bay, cruised south so close to the coast that those on deck were able to watch the progress of an early train from Whitby to Scarborough until the line of illuminated carriages swung away inland to the terminal. At 08:00, just as the master plan demanded, the battle cruisers passed the headland separating the town's North and South Bays and opened fire on their undefended target. The German account, as given by the official historian, owes much to an overheated imagination.

The ships could recognise barbed wire in front of the redoubts of the fortress and also the barracks up the cliff, although the expected fire from the shore was absent. The first salvo from *Derfflinger*'s secondary and tertiary guns struck the cliff. The second flew like birds of prey over the cliffs and landed in the middle of the military installations. Simultaneously, shells from *Von der Tann* could be seen exploding beyond Mount Oliver and high black smoke columns were visible. According to the map there were waterworks there but these could not be seen and indirect fire had to be employed.

At 08:10 the town enjoyed a three-minute respite as the two battle cruisers went about, with *Von der Tann* leading.

The main target for this ship's secondary guns was the gasworks lying 550 metres beyond Mount Oliver. Indirect fire was undertaken and the fall of shot could partially be seen behind the hill. The target of the lighter guns, the railway station, could not be made out because of the haze over the town. Fire was directed at secondary targets for 18 minutes. The observation officer in the foremast could make out a number of direct hits. Beside the Grand Hotel was the coast guard station and this, the signal station on the headland and other installations on the cliffs were taken under effective fire by the *Derfflinger*. One salvo exploded beyond the mole where a large number of fishing vessels lay in the harbour.

The highest British estimate of explosive shells fired into the town was in the region of 500 rounds. The Germans put their ammunition expenditure at 773 rounds. Most of the firing was completely indiscriminate and totally lacking in any form of sensible direction. In total, 17 civilians were killed, including eight women and four children, and over 80 were injured. The ruined castle had taken a pounding and the lighthouse was so severely damaged that it had to be demolished, but the major part of the damage had been inflicted on churches, hotels, shops and private houses. By the standards of World War Two air attacks, it was comparatively minor, consisting of smashed windows, collapsed walls and shattered roofs, most of which was easily repairable. At first, there was a sense of bewilderment, then came the sudden realisation of terrible danger, leading to an exodus from the town by train, motor vehicle, horse and cart and even on foot. The event was totally unexpected and no contingency plans had been prepared to meet it. Fortunately, the panic did not last long, although in its aftermath the post office was besieged as people tried to send telegrams to distant relatives confirming that they were safe. At 08:30 the battle cruisers ceased firing and headed north, working up to a speed of 23 knots. *Kolberg* had played no part in the bombardment and had been forced by heavy seas to lay her mines short of Filey; she was, in fact rolling 12 degrees to port *and* starboard, as well as shipping far more water than was good for her.

Derfflinger and *Von der Tann* arrived off Whitby shortly after 09:00, firing a total of 188 shells at various targets. These included the coast guard station, where the collapse of the signal mast flying a 'battle flag' was greeted with cheers aboard the German ships, the ruined abbey above the town, which lost a little more of its masonry, and the west mole. Accurate observation was impossible because of the narrow, steep-sided valley that enclosed the harbour. Some shells exploded against the cliffs, others far beyond the railway station, their intended target, and a few even landed near the village of Newholm, four miles inland. There was some damage to property, but only three people were killed and two were injured. A great deal of effort had been expended for very little return and at 09:13 the battle cruisers moved off to the north-east.

As the northern bombardment group approached the coast the gale reached its height, ripping funnel smoke to tatters. At about 08:00, with Hartlepool's lighthouse and

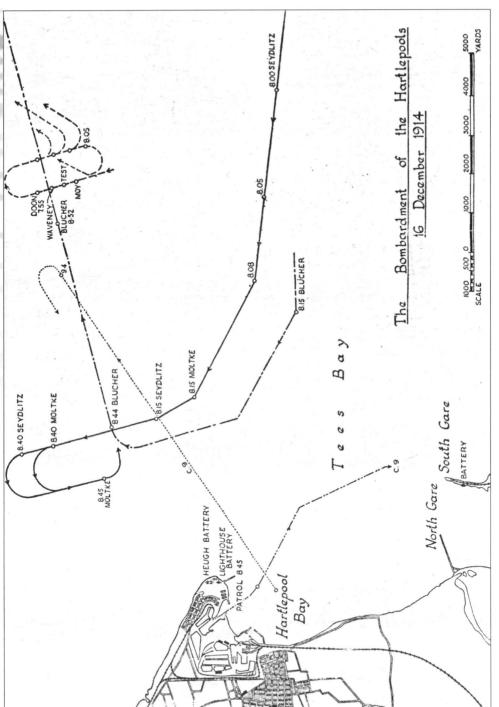

Map 4. The Bombardment of the Hartlepools on 16 December 1914.

49

harbour entrance in sight, the German battle cruisers ran into Fraser's four destroyers approaching from the north. Even if the weather had been favourable, it would have been madness for the smaller ships to engage in a gunnery duel as they were quickly surrounded by fountains of water sent up by a blizzard of exploding shells and raked with splinters that caused a number of casualties and some damage. However, the constant rolling and pounding of the sea made any sort of accurate gunnery impossible even for the battle cruisers, despite the fact that *Moltke* was employing her main as well as secondary armament. Making smoke, the destroyers turned away and after seven minutes disappeared behind their own screen. It would have been normal for them to have retaliated with the only effective weapons at their disposal, their torpedoes, and while there is no mention of this in the British record of the engagement it seems that they did as the Germans were convinced that one destroyer at least had launched torpedoes. Their report states:

> At this moment, to avoid the torpedoes, the German battle cruisers turned north and then north-north-east to veer away from the destroyers, and the Gunnery Officer in the aft conning tower of *Seydlitz* claimed to see a torpedo 20 metres abeam of D Turret, which jumped from the water and then passed aft into the wake. It passed *Moltke* to port. At the same time another torpedo passed close under the bow and a third passed under the stern of *Blücher*.

The principal effect of the action had been to disrupt the German timetable. This dissuaded Hipper from attempting any pursuit and he was becoming uneasy about the opposition he might encounter on the way home. At 08:21 he ordered his ships into their bombardment stations, approximately one-and-a-half miles from the shore.

Meanwhile, the Hartlepool batteries had stood-to at 06:30. The rangefinders and guns were checked over to verify that they were in full working order and after stand-down most of the men went down into the battery shelters. In command were two cousins of German descent, Captain Otto Trechmann at the Heugh Battery and Lieutenant Richard Trechmann at the Lighthouse Battery. Colonel Robson arrived shortly after and told them both of the warning he had received during the night. There was general agreement that while the men should not be alarmed unnecessarily, a sharper lookout than usual should be maintained. Robson then mounted the steps to his command post, from which he continued to scan the horizon, much of which was obscured by patchy fog. Somehow, soldiers have an in-built instinct for trouble, heightened this morning by Robson's unusually early arrival and the fact that he had vanished into the command post. Something, the gunners guessed correctly, was going on. They did not have to wait long to find out what it was.

The rumble of the German guns engaging Fraser's destroyers to the south-east was clearly audible. The gun crews came tumbling up out of their shelters and took post beside their weapons. In the command post the telephone shrilled urgently. Robson snatched up the receiver. The caller was the Port War Signal Station at South Gare, which reported three large warships closing in on the Hartlepools at speed. Robson asked for clarification on their nationality and class. The PWSS not only confirmed that the ships had acknowledged their signal but also that they were Invincible Class battle cruisers and were flying the White Ensign. When asked what they were firing at the PWSS unhelpfully suggested 'the enemy.' Aware that Fraser's destroyers were in the area, Robson requested confirmation that they were not the target. The response of the caller was that he couldn't see what the new arrivals were firing at. The immediate result of this was that the Germans passed right through the South Gare Battery's arc of fire without a shot being fired at them.

There are three points requiring clarification in connection with this exchange. First, the German official history, usually precise as to detail, makes no mention of an exchange of recognition signals with the South Gare PWSS. Second, nor is any mention made of German ships flying the White Ensign. There was no need whatever for the Germans to resort to this ruse, particularly as they were already engaged with the British destroyers. The fact is that both navies flew a white ensign, the difference being that the Royal Navy's was sub-divided into quarters by a red cross while the Imperial German Navy employed a black cross, the respective national emblems being displayed in the left-upper quarter. The claim of a local fisherman to have seen German ships flying a full set of British flags which they replaced with their own when they opened fire does not bear close examination despite gaining popular credence throughout the town. Third, the view from Colonel Robson's command post to the south-east was blocked by the lighthouse and the first he saw of the enemy ships was when they appeared from behind this. They were, however, visible to his two battery commanders, who were steadily tracking their approach with their range-finders and guns.

If mistakes were made by the British, the same was true of the Germans. Their intelligence was seriously out of date, as the primary target for *Seydlitz*, in the lead, were the Cemetery Battery, to the north of the Heugh Battery, and a nearby cable works. The Cemetery Battery had been closed since 1907, although the surrounding area was used for training troops bound for France and did contain a number of trench systems. Next in line was *Moltke*, tasked with neutralising the Lighthouse and Heugh Batteries and the coastguard station on Town Moor. Finally, *Blücher* was to engage factories north of the harbour, the docks and the gas works.

For some minutes the gunners in the two batteries watched as the ships steamed slowly into position off the town. Then, orange flashes along the side of *Seydlitz* signalled that the first broadside had been fired by the battle cruiser's medium and small guns. It landed between the two batteries. Screams accompanied the explosions as several of the Durhams were struck down. All the command post's overhead telephone lines were ripped apart severing Robson's contact with his battery commanders. Almost immediately, *Moltke* and *Blücher* opened fire and the batteries replied.

Few if any of the gunners had been under fire before. Fear obviously existed but it was suppressed by the desperate urge not to let others down and anaesthetised by performing the long familiar drills. All guns, while designed to withstand the enormous pressure of internal propellant explosion, sustain heavy shocks that can affect their fire control equipment, causing time consuming misfires. At various times during the action all three of Hartlepool's guns sustained misfires, but the cause of these was quickly traced and rectified. It was noticed early in the engagement that the enemy was using delayed action high explosive shells. These were ideal for use against ship targets, having been designed to penetrate and explode inside the vessel, but were useless against the batteries concrete works, off which they ricocheted into the town beyond where their explosion caused fires, extensive damage and serious civilian casualties. Within the batteries, the gunners were forced to work in a fog of concrete, brick and plaster dust as well as smoke that sometimes obscured the targets.

On this occasion, however, the enemy was not having it all his own way. *Blücher* was the Lighthouse Battery's target and the official German history describes the damage sustained:

The British coastal guns hit *Blücher* four times. The first was a 6-inch shell which exploded directly beneath the command bridge and put the third and fourth starboard 3.4-inch guns out of action. Of their crews, nine were killed and two seriously wounded. Flying splinters ripped apart the ready-use ammunition. Loose powder, ruined cartridge cases and whole cartridges were blown through the air, fortunately without exploding. The second hit struck the roof of an 8.2-inch gun turret. The turret gun sight and range finder were destroyed by a splinter, but the turret itself remained operational. The third shell struck the side armour below the same turret, without effect. The fourth struck the upper edge of the foremast observation platform, ripping away aerials as well as damaging signal and searchlight equipment.

Some observers have suggested that immediately after the first hit, *Blücher* appeared to veer off course towards a known shoal before recovering. As the command bridge was directly above the explosion, we shall never know, as the ship's log was lost, along with *Blücher* herself, some months later.

In Captain Otto Trechmann's Heugh Battery the policy was to concentrate the fire of both guns on a single ship, in this case *Seydlitz*. The official German account has it that fire from the Cemetery Battery (sic) was falling 100 to 200 metres short but admits that at about 08:37, when the Germans effected a change of course, the Heugh Battery scored three hits in rapid succession.

The first struck the forecastle and wrecked several ventilation shafts and lockers. A great deal of water poured in through the hole, although this was quickly closed with wood. The second shell passed through the outer mantle of the fore funnel, two metres above the deck, and exploded in the inner sleeve, making a hole four to five metres in size. The third shell hit the ventilation shaft of the after superstructure and damaged searchlight cables and equipment. Several life jackets caught fire and splinters penetrated the low-pressure turbine room, but only one man was slightly wounded.

As *Seydlitz* drew away the Heugh Battery shifted its fire to the *Moltke*, obtaining a hit that caused a heavy explosion forward, wrecking a number of cabins. Furious, the ship's commander, Captain von Levetzow, brought his main armament into action on the grounds that it would be easier to spot the big guns' fall of shot. His subsequent claim to have silenced the Heugh Battery has not the slightest basis in fact.

Another element now entered the battle. The lookouts in the foretops of *Seydlitz* and *Moltke* could see the masts and funnels of the old light cruisers *Patrol* and *Forward* moving towards the harbour entrance. This unwelcome development was not visible to those in the ships' lower conning towers and gun positions. The harbour entrance was therefore brought under continuous fire. *Patrol*, commanded by Captain Alan Bruce, was in the lead. She was assisted by tugs as she negotiated the dog-leg to reach the exit from the Victoria Dock, but these cast off as she reached the Old Pier and began to pick up speed. She was cheered by those nearby who knew that she was hopelessly outgunned and was going to her death with the sole intention of inflicting as much damaged as possible on her powerful opponents.

Fortunately, it did not come to that. An 11-inch shell from the *Moltke* exploded aboard, killing several men and wounding others. *Blücher* had also resorted to using her main armament, one round of which blasted a hole low down in the hull through which water began to flood. Bruce had just ordered 'Full Ahead,' but now he was left with no alternative but to run the ship aground beside the main channel. As the tidal state was at its lowest, this presented no difficulty, although it left insufficient room for *Forward* to pass.

However, Lieutenant C.L.Y. Dering, commanding the submarine *C-9*, had no intention of being left stranded inside the harbour. Despite there being only nine feet of water beside *Patrol*, he managed to squeeze his little craft past although she scraped along the bottom with her propeller churning up clouds of silt. Once in open water, there was very little chance of her torpedoes finding a target, and in any event she would have to remain surfaced to fire them, exposed to destruction by innumerable guns. Even submerged, the concussive effect of a salvo from the enemy's main armament would be sufficient to inflict critical damage on the little craft. Nevertheless, this was the lesser of the two evils and Dering headed south to put *C-9* on the bottom off Seaton Carew. Once things had quietened down, he brought her to the surface to find not a German warship in sight. This led to the only glimmer of humour to emerge from a very grim morning indeed. During the next few days the submarine's crew informed people that as soon as *C-9* put in an appearance, the enemy had realised that the game was up and promptly headed for home!

There is some doubt as to whether Hipper even saw *C-9*'s conning tower emerging from the harbour entrance. Having completed his mission, he was more concerned with rejoining the southern element of his group and making his way home. His ships turned away from the coast to fade into the mist. As soon as the tide had risen sufficiently, *Forward* was sent out to look for them and report their position, but there was no trace of them.

The raiders left behind a chaos of wrecked and burning buildings and the horror of bodies sprawled in the streets. Many people tried to escape by train or other means, just as they did in Scarborough. In addition to the naval casualties sustained aboard *Doon* and *Patrol*, two RGA gunners were killed, as was one soldier of the Royal Engineers and six infantrymen of the Durham Light Infantry, a further eleven of whom were wounded. It was, however, the civilian casualties that shocked most. One hundred and twelve people were either killed during the bombardment itself or died from their injuries.

Of these, 32 were women and 37 were children. Material damage was widespread and confirmed that, as at Scarborough, much of the German gunnery had been

Dreadnought battleships of Admiral Sir John Jellicoe's Grand Fleet at sea. The fleet's battle squadrons were generally eight strong and sailed in parallel columns. By turning to port or starboard as required, this enabled them to form a line of battle very quickly. (IWM Q18121)

Battleships of the German High Seas Fleet were also formed into eight-strong battle squadrons, sub-divided into two equal divisions. When at sea, the fleet preferred the line-ahead formation for tactical reasons based on its escape from a superior force. The manoeuvre was known as the *Gefechtskehrtwendung* or Battle Turn-About, which involved every ship in the line reversing course simultaneously away from the enemy. The leading ship is possibly the *Helgoland*, a dreadnought completed in 1909. The Imperial Navy made extensive use of Zeppelin rigid airships for scouting purposes, but these operations were not always successful. Admiral Reinhard Scheer, the fleet's penultimate commander, once expressed a wish that they would tell him where the British were rather than where they weren't!

At Jutland the High Seas Fleet included three battle squadrons of which the Second consisted entirely of old pre-dreadnought battleships, led by the *Deutschland*, which had actually served as fleet flagship until 1912. Her armament consisted of four 11-inch guns, fourteen 6.7-inch guns and twenty 3.4-inch guns. The secondary armament ammunition was so heavy that mechanical assistance was required to handle it, resulting in a slow rate of fire. She is seen here at gunnery practice on a calm day, firing what appears to be a full broadside.

HMS *Lion* in 1914 with an inset photo of Beatty.

The light cruiser HMS *Birmingham* in 1913.

HMS *Lion*.

HMS *Lion*.

HMS *Southampton*.

HMS *Queen Mary*.

The attack on undefended Scarborough created such shock and anger that a surge in the armed services' recruiting was the immediate result. Typical of the recruiting posters produced shortly after the event was this painting by E. Kemp-Welch.

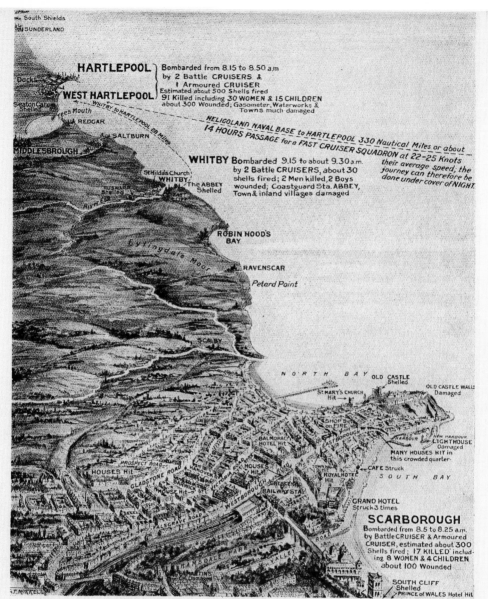

Scarboro' Under Fire

MERCILESS DESCENT OF DEATH AND DESTRUCTION.

Defenceless Town Sacrificed to German "Kultur."

FUSILLADE OF 500 SHELLS.

Men, Women, and Children Killed.

Oblique picture maps were a popular method of describing the course of an action to the general public. Not a great deal has changed since this example was drawn, although the Scarborough–Whitby railway fell a victim to Dr Beeching's axe and has long been lifted. The commentary is not altogether accurate but provides the reader with a reasonable summary of events.

A general view of Scarborough's South Bay during the bombardment. The large building to the left of centre is the Grand Hotel, which sustained several hits. The castle is on the headland to the right. Below it is the small fishing harbour. In his excitement the editor of the *Berliner Lokalenanzeiger* displayed his ignorance of British geography by describing Scarborough as 'the most important harbour on the ease coast of England between the Humber and the Thames.'

A drawing for the *Illustrated London News* by S. Begg showing shells striking the Grand Hotel's restaurant on the sea front. More shells can be seen exploding near the ruined castle and among the houses of the town.

A watercolour by James Clark painted shortly after the engagement shows the scene on Hartlepool waterfront just after the German warships had opened fire, inflicting casualties on the infantrymen of the Durham Light Infantry. The Lighthouse Battery, on the right of the picture, is replying and smoke from the guns of the Heugh Battery is drifting across the scene from the left.

Some of Hipper's ships, including the battle cruisers *Derfflinger* and *Von Der Tann* and the armoured cruiser *Blucher*, on their way home after the bombardment. Hipper was unaware that he had been abandoned by the rest of the High Seas Fleet which had returned to harbour following a skirmish with British destroyers. The photograph was taken from the light cruiser *Kolberg*, the bridge of which had been stove in by heavy seas.

     ↑ "Blücher"   "Indomitable" ↑   From a drawing by Montague Dawson

The Sinking of the German Cruiser, "Blücher," on January 24, 1915

The German vessel was one of those which took part in the action of the battle cruisers on Sunday, January 24, 1915. She was the last of the retreating German line, and came under heavy fire. She finally rolled over to port, and her men scrambled over the side in a great crowd. Many were rescued by the British boats and became prisoners of war in England. Some of the " Blücher's" twelve 8-in. guns can be seen pointing skywards as the vessel rolled over

A contemporary sketch by the artist Montague Dawson for *The Sphere* magazine showing the last moments of the *Blucher* with *Indomitable* steaming past in pursuit of the German battle cruisers. Attempts by British destroyers to rescue the *Blucher*'s survivors had to be abandoned when the destroyers themselves came under attack from an enemy Zeppelin and a seaplane. (*The Mary Evans Picture Library*)

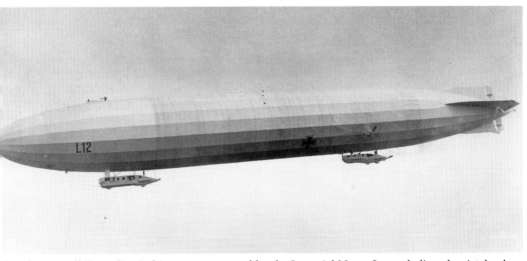

Most, but not all Zeppelin airships were operated by the Imperial Navy. It was believed, mistakenly, that by bombing targets in England they would break the civilians' will to continue the war. This excellent study of Zeppelin *L12* seem so have been taken as the ship was about to land, hence the cable seen dangling directly in front of the forward control gondola. A machine gun post for local defence is situated on top of the envelope. (*IWM Q.58455*)

L12 was not a lucky ship. On the night of 9/10 August, in company with Zeppelins *L9*, *L10*, *L11* and *L13*, it set out to bomb London. In a typical demonstration of the Zeppelins' poor navigational qualities, *L9* attacked Goole, *L10* unloaded its bombs over Eastchurch airfield and the Thames, *L11*'s Captain thought that Lowestoft was Harwich and dropped all his bombs in the sea, and *L13* turned for home with engine trouble. *L12* arrived over Westcliffe-on-Sea believing that it was Great Yarmouth, was caught in searchlight beams, engaged by anti-aircraft guns and chased into the clouds by an Avro 504b fighter. It was again engaged by anti-aircraft guns over Dover and was brought down with a broken back into the sea between Ostend and Zeebrugge. The wreck was towed ashore by a German destroyer and broken up. (*IWM Q.20358*)

The Zeppelins were expensive to produce and the results they produced in the strategic bomber role were disappointing. As the war progressed this role was increasingly taken over by the Imperial German Air Service's Gotha and Staaken heavy bombers. This example is a Gotha Vb, manned by a crew of three and powered by two 250-hp Mercedes engines. It had a maximum speed of 87.5 mph and could reach a height of 19,500 feet. Its normal bomb load was one 500lb bomb with local

defence supplied to two 7.9mm machine guns. In their day, these aircraft considered to be monsters of their kind. (*IWM Q.67123*)

One of the High Seas Fleet's battle squadrons making the *Gefechtskehrtwendung* or Battle Turn-About during the Battle of Jutland, photographed from a Zeppelin. Despite the naturally murky conditions of the evening, huge quantities of funnel smoke help to obscure the detail, but what was taking place is perfectly clear. This manoeuvre carried with it a high risk of collision and reflected the defeatist German view of any major encounter with the Grand Fleet, but at Jutland it saved the High Seas Fleet from destruction twice.

The badly battered battle cruiser *Seydlitz* undergoing repair at Wilhelmshaven. If she had had to travel just a few more miles before reaching home there is no doubt that she would have foundered. As it was, her bows were almost awash and she was drawing 44 feet of water forward and listing heavily to port. With assistance from two pumping vessels she managed to stay afloat but in an attempt to lighten her the roof and some armour plate was removed from A turret, which was also stripped of its two 11-inch guns. Even then, it was necessary for the tug *Albatross* to drag her stern first across the Jade Bar. Her repairs were not completed until 16 September, three-and-a-half months after the battle. Despite being a great favourite of the German public, she never fought again. (*IWM SP.2159*)

S. M. S. „Seydlitz" nach der Skagerrak-Schlacht
schweren Treffern in der Schleuse zu Wilhelmshaven.

A fine-looking and superficially invulnerable ship armed with eight 13.5-inch and sixteen 4-inch guns, the battle cruiser *Queen Mary* gets under way. At Jutland she served in the 1st Battle Cruiser Squadron. Unfortunately, on British battle cruisers the danger of fire from an explosion within a turret spreading to the magazine below had not been eliminated, as it had on German battle cruiser and some battleships.

Literally, gone in a flash. Some 29,700 tons of steel and armour plate vanish in a cloud of flame and smoke as flash penetrates one of *Queen Mary*'s magazines. Only eight men survived from a ship's company of 1,266.

German shells overfly HMS *Malaya* during the Battle of Jutland.

Jutland hero Boy Cornwell.

HMS *Chester* at Jutland. (*Wylie*)

Damage to HMS *Southampton* after Jutland.

Jutland 2.00pm. HMS *Barham* leading the 5th Battle Squadron.

The 2nd Battle Squadron at Jutland.

indiscriminate. Some 300 houses and small shops had sustained damage, as had hospitals, churches and schools. The January 1915 edition of *The Engineer* recorded damage that could be considered of military significance.

> Three gasometers went up in flames. A water tower and the engine house of the gasworks were partially destroyed. A timber yard and granary at the port along with valuable raw materials were set ablaze. The dockyard of Richardson, Westgard, Roper and Company suffered particularly, as did the installations of the Irving Shipping Company at Middleton. Administration buildings, revolving cranes and assembly shops were likewise badly damaged and partly destroyed by fire. Two ships under construction in the latter yard were hit several times by shells and on one the sternpost was blown off. The new steamer *Sagoma River*, tied up near a shed, and the steamers *Fair Field* and *City of Newcastle* were badly damaged. The steamer *Denebola*, which was in the harbour basin, was also hit. Other shells struck railway buildings and tore up the track.

For Hipper, the most dangerous phase of the operation had just begun. At about 11:00 his combined force entered the western end of the minefield gap. It was obvious that he would take this route home and while Beatty was heading to close the gap from its northern end Warrender was doing likewise to the south. At 11:25 Beatty's cruisers, operating to the north of his battle cruisers, encountered the light cruisers Hipper had detached some hours earlier, which were now well on their way home. Beatty, however, was after Hipper and ordered two of the four cruisers to break contact and resume the search for the German battle cruisers. Unfortunately, his signal was corrupted in passing and the entire cruiser squadron broke off the engagement. For their part, the German cruisers turned away and headed south.

By noon, Hipper was halfway through the minefield, little suspecting that he was approaching a trap. At 12:15 the German cruisers became visible to Warrender through the mist and he set off to the north-east to intercept them in the belief that Hipper was nearby. Having been advised of this development, Hipper turned south-east, hoping to draw Warrender away from the cruisers. Beatty, thinking that Hipper had slipped past him, turned east at 12:30. Having been alerted to the presence of British battleships to the south, he swung away northwards at 12:45. Warrender, meanwhile, had lost the enemy cruisers in the mist and had turned west five minutes earlier.

The pursuit had now entered its most crucial phase. Beatty had read Hipper's mind correctly and turned north at 13:15. He was on a converging course with Hipper and would have come within sight of his ships shortly after. Warrender had also turned north at 13:24. Hipper would almost certainly have found himself in serious trouble had not Beatty received a signal from the Admiralty, based on radio intercepts. It told him that the enemy was heading south-east, and that left him with no choice but to turn east in an attempt to get between Hipper and his base. He found nothing but continued to search until 15:17, when the hunt was called off. Investigation of the signal revealed that it was not based on real time (i.e. as events were happening) but on the situation that had existed between 12:15 and 12:45.

Poor visibility, bad signals procedure and sheer good luck had all helped Hipper to make good his escape, although he was not quite out of danger yet. As his battle cruiser approached the German coast early on 17 December, they encountered the submarine *E-11*, part of a four-strong patrol line established by Commodore R.J.B. Keyes, of whom more in due course, running north from the mouth of the Weser. Commanded by Lieutenant Commander M.E. Naismith, one of the war's submarine aces, *E-11* fired a torpedo which passed under its target because of a design fault. She was then forced to dive to avoid being rammed. In doing so she lost her trim and in returning to the attack surfaced involuntarily. Startled, Hipper's ships scattered but finally straggled into port.

It was not the sort of dignified entrance any admiral would have preferred, but Hipper was now a national hero. He had, after all, carried out his mission in difficult conditions and brought his ships home with minimal casualties and damage. The German and Austrian press made much of his success and the apparent failings of the Royal Navy. Ingenohl also received credit as the fleet commander but some senior officers, notably Tirpitz, were highly critical of him, claiming that by his hurried return to port he had forfeited a significant victory. Hipper was less pointed in his reaction although he had clearly not enjoyed being left to fend for himself. There were also bitter comments that Ingenohl had allowed the High Seas Fleet to be chased back into its harbours by handful of British destroyers, but these were below the belt and took no account of the fact that Ingenohl was bound by the Kaiser's strict order not to become involved in a fleet action.

Meanwhile, back in Hartlepool, Robson's political instincts had led him to assemble the personnel of both batteries for a group photograph on the afternoon of the bombardment. The result suggests that it was a cold day as most of the officers have pulled on their short 'warm' overcoats. The men, on the other hand, are wearing their normal service dress and are as smartly turned out as if they were about to mount a ceremonial guard. Their expressions are inscrutable and one suspects that they would prefer to be giving what help they could in the town, where many of their families lived. Only when the shutter had clicked were they formed into working parties and detailed to assist in the clearing up. The following morning they were paraded and a congratulatory letter from Lord Kitchener was read to them. A number of decorations were awarded as a result of the action, the first of its kind since the Dutch Wars of the

Seventeenth Century, if one discounts a comic opera landing by French troops near Fishguard in 1797. Robson became a Companion of the Distinguished Service Order, for although he had remained isolated in his command post during the fighting, it was thanks to his efforts that the two batteries were as well disciplined and efficient as they were. Sergeant T. Douthwaite received a Distinguished Conduct Medal for removing and making safe a misfired cartridge from the gun in the Lighthouse Battery, contrary to the standard safety drill, so that the battery could remain in action. Sergeant F.W. Mallin and Acting Bombardier J.J. Hope, the gun captains of the Heugh Battery, were awarded the Military Medal. It was expected that as the two battery commanders the Trechmanns' part in the action would be acknowledged in some way, but it was not. The probable reason was the priggish attitude common at this phase, that junior officers should not expect to be rewarded simply for carrying out their duties. The obvious unfairness of their treatment led to it being brought to the attention of Winston Churchill, but as it was an Army rather than a Navy matter he could not intervene, and there it rested. The Royal Navy received no awards at all, although the Hartlepool and District Traders Defence Association presented an Address to the ships based in the port praising their immense courage in attempting to tackle their huge opponents.

The British public, however, was angry that the Royal Navy had allowed the raid to happen and angrier still that the Germans had been allowed to get away with it, although it remained in ignorance of most of the facts, including the part that luck had played in the enemy's escape. It was furious at the unprovoked slaughter of innocent civilians of all ages, regarding this as an extension of the 'frighfulness' displayed by the German Army in its march across Belgium. Their prompt execution of civilians who took pot-shots at the troops was understandable, but not the destruction of entire communities as a reprisal, as had happened at Louvain, where the ancient university and its priceless library were burned to the ground. Nor was there any doubt that there were occasions when the troops were out of hand because their officers made them march hard and allowed them to drink hard as a reward. Looting, rapes and attacks on civilians were far from being isolated incidents, but in many cases the worst of the atrocities attributed to the German Army had no foundation. Even so, Germany's reputation as a civilised nation was taking a serious battering, largely because those in charge simply did not understand the importance of good public relations and were therefore at an immediate disadvantage in what today is known as psywar. The reverse was true in Great Britain, where it was grudgingly accepted that while the Hartlepools had sustained by far the worst casualties and damage, they were defended and, since they also played an important part in the nation's war effort, they were a legitimate target. Scarborough, on the other hand, was simply a holiday resort and nothing could justify the indiscriminate killing that had taken place. The outrage received the fullest publicity at home and abroad and an effective poster campaign proved to be a major boost to recruiting with it simple message: Remember Scarborough! The reaction of neutral countries, especially that of the United States, where a high percentage of immigrant Germans had made their home, was sufficiently cool to produce a more sober reflection among the less strident element of the Berlin press.

Back in the United Kingdom the criticism of the Royal Navy had been taken seriously to heart. Beatty's answer to the problem was characteristically simple and straightforward – move the battle cruisers and their supporting squadron of battleships from Caithness to Rosyth and the time taken to reach the operational area would be halved.

CHAPTER 7

Once Too Often –
The Battle of Dogger Bank

In the view of the German Admiralty the foreign criticism of the raids on Scarborough, Whitby and the Hartlepools was something for the diplomats to deal with while the Imperial Navy got on with the war. During the first weeks of January 1915 Rear Admiral Eckermann, the High Seas Fleet's Chief of Staff, believed that British light forces were carrying out an increased level of patrolling in the area of Dogger Bank. Encouraged by the successful outcome of the previous month's operation, he urged Ingenohl to disrupt these using the fast battle cruisers. The fleet commander, however, was less than enthusiastic about the idea as Hipper's fighting strength had been considerably reduced by the decision to dock *Von de Tann* for refitting. Nevertheless, Eckermann was importunate in pressing his idea until Ingernohl finally gave way, instructing Hipper by radio to examine the Dogger Bank area at dawn on 24 January, assess the nature of the enemy's operations and engage the British presence.

At 17:45 on 23 January, therefore, Hipper emerged from the Jade anchorage with *Seyditz*, *Moltke*, *Derfflinger* and *Blücher*, the light cruisers *Graudenz*, *Rostock*, *Stralsund* and *Kolberg*, the heavy weather damage sustained by the last during the December operation having been repaired. Also present was a screening force of nineteen destroyers. Unknown to Hipper, Beatty's 1st Battle Cruiser Squadron, consisting of *Lion*, *Tiger* and *Princess Royal*, Rear Admiral Moore's 2nd Battle Cruiser Squadron with the slower *New Zealand* and *Indomitable*, and Commodore Goodenough's 1st Light Cruiser Squadron weighed anchor only minutes later and sailed for a rendezvous, timed for 08:00 near Dogger Bank, with a force of cruisers and destroyers based at Harwich under Commodore Reginald Tyrwhitt. Unfortunately for the Germans, the Admiralty's radio intercept operators in Room 40 has listened with interest to the most recent exchange between Ingenohl and Hipper, with the result that the latter was actually sailing into a trap. The wisdom of Beatty's moving his battle cruisers south to Rosyth now became apparent as they rapidly closed the gap separating them from their opponents.

At first light next morning *Kolberg*, steaming to port of the main body of the battle cruiser fleet, spotted a strange cruiser coming up from the south. The stranger was the light cruiser *Aurora*, part of the Harwich force. She flashed an unfamiliar recognition signal, to which *Kolberg* replied by opening fire, scoring two hits. *Aurora* responded at once and also began scoring hits. Aboard *Seydlitz*, his flagship, Hipper ordered a general turn toward the firing in the belief that he had found the British light forces that Eckermann had reported to Ingernohl. Hardly had the turn been completed than *Stralsund*, to starboard of the battle cruisers, reported a large quantity of smoke approaching from the north-north-west. Believing that its origin was British battleships, Hipper was not unduly concerned as he knew he could outrun them, but it continued to approach at speed and was closing fast. By the time the range had closed to 25,000 yards he suddenly realised that he had Beatty's much faster battle cruisers on his hands. At 07:35 he gave the order to head for home.

What followed was a stern chase in which the Germans were at an immediate disadvantage. Hipper's slowest ship was the *Blücher*, capable of 23 knots, and some of his coal-fired destroyers were no better. The three ships in Beatty's squadron worked up to 27 knots and although Moore's squadron was a little slower the Germans were being steadily overhauled. The British battle cruisers were echeloned to the left rear with *Lion* leading, then *Tiger*, then *Princess Royal*, then *New Zealand* and finally *Indomitable*, so that they did not obscure each other's targets during the pursuit. Likewise, Beatty ordered his lighter ships not to penetrate the space between the opposing battle cruisers because their smoke would obscure the target. Even in 1915, using the wind was as important as it had been in Nelson's time. As Hipper's line was to port of Beatty's, the north-easterly wind would blow the Germans' funnel and gub smoke in the direction of their target, and an intervening screen laid by destroyers was quickly dispersed. Conversely, the British smoke would be blown clear to starboard, leaving the enemy ships in full view. At 08:52 *Lion* opened fire at 20,000 yards, followed by the rest of Beatty's battle cruisers as they closed the range. Hipper's ships were running in the order *Seydlitz*, *Moltke*, *Derfflinge* and *Blücher*. After several salvos had been fired, *Blücher* was straddled at 09:00 and received repeated hits as she was overtaken by the leading ships in Beatty's line, but it was not until 09:11 that the German guns, with their shorter range, could begin to reply.

At this point, with the British steadily drawing level with their opponents, Beatty's command and control of the battle began to fall apart. He ordered his ships to engage their opposite numbers in the enemy line, intending this to be interpreted from the front with *New Zealand* and *Indomitable* both engaging *Blücher* at the rear. Unfortunately, Captain H.B. Pelly, commanding *Tiger*, interpreted the instruction in precisely the opposite way. This meant that *Lion* and *Tiger* were both firing at *Seydlitz*, no one was firing at *Moltke*, *Princess Royal* was firing first at *Blücher* and then at *Derfflinger*, and *New Zealand* and *Indomitable* were both firing at *Blücher* as they came up. What made matters worse was that the recently commissioned *Tiger* had not completed her gunnery trials, a process sorely needed as her gunnery officer was so bad that he treated *Lion*'s shell splashes as his own, which were three miles beyond their intended target. *Tiger*'s contribution to the battle, therefore, amounted to very little.

Nevertheless, at 09:40 a shell from *Lion* penetrated the barbette of *Seydlitz*'s D turret and exploded, setting fire to propellant charges waiting to be loaded. The flames not only roared up into the turret and down into the magazine, but also through a connecting door to C turret that should have been closed. Only prompt flooding of both magazines saved the ship from being blown apart, but 165 men died a horrible death in the inferno.

Lion was herself taking steady punishment from the concentrated fire directed at her and at 09:40 received several hits from a salvo fired by *Derfflinger*. The worst of these contaminated her port feed tank with sea water and she began to take a list to port. The port engine had to be stopped and as her speed fell away to 15 knots she was overtaken by *Tiger* and *Princess Royal*. In total, *Lion* sustained 14 hits one of which penetrated A turret and caused an ammunition fire which was fortunately extinguished before it could spread. *Lion*'s generators were also put out of action, leaving her signal lamps without power, and her radio antennae had been shot away, as had all but two of her flag hoists, which now remained Beatty's sole remaining means of communicating with his command.

At 10:54 there occurred one of those unexpected incidents that can affect the course of battles. Beatty thought he saw a submarine periscope off *Lion*'s starboard bow and ordered a 90 degree turn to port to avoid entering a U-boat trap. This may have been a torpedo that had run its course and surfaced when its fuel was exhausted, having been launched by a German destroyer earlier in the engagement. Whatever the truth, Beatty now realised that the turn ordered would increase the range between his ships and the enemy. He therefore decided to halve the turn to 45 degrees by signalling 'Course NE.' By now, *Lion* was trailing well behind his other ships and to clarify his intentions he decided to repeat Nelson's signal, 'Engage the enemy more closely.' This had been deleted from the signal book and replaced with 'Attack the rear of the enemy.' Both signals went up at the same time reading, 'Attack the rear of the enemy course NE.' In the present circumstances, this was gibberish and could only have referred to the *Blücher*, which Hipper had abandoned to her fate and was being steadily battered into a wreck.

It was now up to Beatty's Second-in-Command, Rear Admiral Moore, to recognise the fact and use his initiative by maintaining the pursuit of the enemy. Instead, he decided to stick to the Navy's code of strict obedience to orders and concentrated all his efforts into sending *Blücher* to the bottom. The lowest estimate of hits sustained by the cruiser was 50, the highest 70. *Blücher* fought to the bitter end, scoring two hits with her main armament on the British battle cruisers and damaging the destroyer *Meteor* so badly that she had to be taken in tow. The *coup de grace* was administered by *Aurora* with two torpedoes. Reducing to a blazing wreck, *Blücher* turned over on her beam ends and finally sank at 12:07. Of her 792-strong crew, only 237 were picked up by British destroyers. The number would have been greater had not a patrolling Zeppelin, L5, and a German seaplane attacked the rescuers with their bombs and machine guns, forcing them to abandon their efforts.

Beatty had transferred his flag to the destroyer *Attack* but by the time he caught up with the battle Hipper's remaining ships had increased their lead so much that any further pursuit had become pointless. He turned for home with the heavily damaged *Lion* under tow by the *Indomitable*. He had scored an undoubted success in which the enemy had lost a major unit and sustained over 1,000 casualties, whereas no British ships had been lost and casualties amounted to only 15 killed and 32 wounded.

Naturally, both sides held an inquest into what had taken place. The Kaiser's fury knew no bounds as he raged against admirals who committed his ships to action before his soldiers had won the war, a prospect that seemed well within the bounds of possibility for a while. Ingernohl and Eckermann were sacked immediately, the former being replaced by Admiral Hugo von Pohl, an unpopular, arrogant individual in poor health who strongly advocated submarine warfare and in particular a U-boat blockade of the United Kingdom in preference to surface operations involving the High Seas Fleet. Such a change of policy outraged Tirpitz, who objected strongly to his creation being sidelined, but he lacked experience of active command and people were becoming very tired of his plotting, so he was sidelined himself. For the Imperial Navy, the one good thing to come out of Dogger Bank was that when *Seydlitz* was repaired the open trunking between turrets and magazines was equipped with doors that closed automatically once the shell and charge had passed upwards from the magazine. The same modification was applied to the rest of the battle cruisers and some battleships. Likewise, dangerous ammunition-handling procedures were eliminated. These defects also existed in similar British ships and would become horribly apparent the following year. The German operational analysis also accepted that Beatty's regular appearance whenever Hipper put to sea was no accident, but remained unaware that their wireless codes were in British hands. After some discussion, it was decided that a British agent was active in the area of Jade Bay and possessed the means to transmit his findings to England.

On the British side, Beatty believed that he had been robbed of a major victory. He could not blame Moore openly as his Second-in-Command had simply carried out his own specific orders, although a display of initiative on Moore's part might have produced results. On the other hand, it might not. Leaving the destruction of *Blücher* aside, German main armament gunnery had scored 22 hits with heavy calibre shells, including 16 on *Lion*, whereas the British battle cruisers had scored only seven, albeit that these had produced devastating results. The possibility existed, therefore, that if the engagement had continued the British could have sustained further serious damage and even lost a ship or two, given *Tiger*'s wretched performance. Against this, Hipper was running short of ammunition and was not interested in prolonging the engagement. A difficult situation was resolved when Moore was posted away from the Grand Fleet to less exacting duties, without loss of rank. Further operational analysis resulted in a better target allocation system and the issue of emergency radios to replace those that might be damaged in action.

These matters apart, a new dimension had entered the battle for the North Sea. The senior officers of the Imperial Navy's air arm believed that the bombs dropped by their Zeppelin airships on targets in England would inflict more damage on civilian morale than periodic raids by the High Seas Fleet, and in the week prior to Dogger Bank had carried out a raid against Sherringham, Kings Lynn and Yarmouth with Zeppelins L3 and L4. Four people were killed, 13 were injured and several houses were damaged. It was known that the Germans used their airships for naval reconnaissance, but deliberately targeting civilians from the air was regarded as just another example of the enemy's 'frightfulness.' The ability to shock had been lost during the attacks on Scarborough, Whitby and the Harlepools, and attitudes to the enemy had hardened even further. What did cause concern was the apparent lack of defence against this form of attack, a deficiency which had to be remedied quickly.

CHAPTER 8

Scheer Strikes Back

For the High Seas Fleet, the immediate consequence of the failure at Dogger Bank was that, for the moment, all but a handful of offensive operations became the responsibility of the submarine branch. With effect from 4 February 1915 all merchant vessels in British waters, including those of neutrals, were at risk of being attacked by U-boats. The United States promptly lodged an objection to such a policy, despite which the American tanker *Gulflight* was sunk on 1 May with the loss of two of her crew. On 7 May the British liner *Lusitania* was torpedoed and sunk without warning off the southern coast of Ireland. No less than 1,189 passengers and crew lost their lives, including 124 Americans. Although feelings ran high in the United States, it was generally accepted that the strong diplomatic protest delivered lost some of its force as a result of the German Embassy in Washington having issued a prior public warning that Americans should not travel aboard the ship. Again, in addition to her passengers, *Lusitania* was carrying a war cargo that included a quantity of small arms, ammunition and bullion. However, when four more Americans died when another British liner, the *Arabic*, was sunk on 19 August, there were no such mitigating factors and such was the fury generated in the United States that the German Admirals were forced to abandon the 'unrestricted' aspect of the submarine campaign, instructing its U-boats that they must only deliver their attacks on the surface. Despite this, yet more American deaths resulted from the torpedoing of the cross-Channel ferry *Sussex* on 24 March 1916. Washington's reaction stopped just short of an ultimatum and, to avoid the United States' probable entry into the war, the submarine campaign was abandoned the following month. This process was made a little easier by Pohl's death on 23 February and his replacement by Admiral Reinhard Scheer, who felt that the High Seas Fleet should be making a greater contribution to the war.

While no major surface operations had taken place in the North Sea since Dogger Bank, there was constant naval activity that included patrolling, mine-laying and mine-sweeping. By the spring of 1915 the northern entrance to and exit from the North Sea was being permanently patrolled by the Royal Navy's 10th Cruiser Squadron which consisted of no less than 26 armed merchant cruisers. These were medium-sized merchant vessels 'taken up from trade' as the ancient wording of the requisition put it, well-enough armed with guns to give a good account of themselves if they ran into trouble. In 1915 they intercepted no less than 2,555 vessels of various nationalities, 743 of which were sent in for detailed investigation; in 1916 the figures were, respectively, 3,390 and 889.

Another type of vessel, the Q ship, was also entering service. They were small, harmless-looking craft that might resemble a tramp steamer or a schooner. When a U-boat surfaced nearby, some of the crew would enact a panic and run to lower their boats. The Q ship would then unmask its cleverly concealed guns and reduce the U-boat to a sinking wreck before its own crew could man their deck gun. Naturally, when taken aboard, the German survivors complained that this was not playing the game.

The German equivalent of the armed merchant cruiser was the commerce raider. Again, these were medium-sized merchantmen, generally mounting a heavier concealed armament than their opponents, and they had the ability to change their appearance quickly to match genuine vessels listed in Lloyd's Register of Shipping. Most of their kills took place far from the North Sea, the most successful being *Moewe*, a former banana boat that was credited with sinking 122,000 tons of Allied shipping; *Wolf*, a former liner, was credited with 120,000 tons; and *Seeadler*, a harmless looking sailing ship that sank 18,000 tons. For fuel and rations, these and other raiders lived off their victims before sending them to the bottom.

On the morning of 8 August 1915 one such raider, the *Meteor* commanded by Captain von Knorr, was returning to Germany after laying a minefield in the Moray Firth. Flying the Russian merchant flag, she was pursued by *The Ramsay* (sic), a 1,600-ton armed boarding vessel that in peacetime had conveyed holiday makers from Liverpool to the Isle of Man. She ordered the *Meteor* to stop and prepared to send a boarding party across. Down came the Russian flag, up went the German ensign, hatches clanged open to reveal the muzzles of guns that opened fire immediately, and four minutes later, having additionally been hit by a torpedo, *The Ramsay* was on her way to the bottom. Knorr picked up her survivors, supplied them with tobacco and held a funeral service for those who had died. The *Meteor* was run down by a light cruiser and scuttled before she could reach home, with Knorr making certain that his British passengers were picked up while he and his men made good their escape in a commandeered Swedish fishing boat.

Another raider to be caught was the *Greif* (Vulture), armed with four 5.9-inch guns and two torpedo tubes. She left the Elbe on 27 February 1916 following an unfortunate blaze of publicity arising from a personal visit by the Kaiser's brother, Prince Henry of Prussia. She was also sighted by a British submarine and clandestine radio traffic to the effect that a commerce raider was leaving the Skagerrak may all have contributed to her destruction. At 09:15 on 29 February she sailed straight into a carefully set trap to the north-east of the Shetlands.

Stopped by the armed merchant cruiser *Alcantara*, she identified herself as the Norwegian *Rena*, on passage between La Plata and Trondheim. Although her appearance corresponded with that of the *Rena* it was decided to send over a boarding party. As the boat was being hoisted out a signal was received from another armed merchant cruiser, the *Andes*, some fourteen miles distant, to the effect that *Greif* was the ship they were looking for. This was almost certainly listened to by the enemy's radio operator, for *Greif* opened fire immediately, wrecking the boat and seriously damaging *Alcantara*'s steering.

The raider had chosen a bad opponent, for *Alcantara*'s commander, Captain T.E. Wardle, had not only made her the best gunnery ship in the 10th Cruiser Squadron, she had already cleared for action. Round after round was slammed into the German raider until her guns were silenced, her upper works were ablaze and she was seriously down by the bows. Through the smoke, her crew could be seen taking to such boats as remained. Clearly, she was doomed for *Andes* was heading for the scene at full speed, followed by the cruiser *Comus* and the destroyer *Munster*. Unfortunately, *Alcantara* had also sustained a mortal wound, almost certainly from one of the enemy's torpedoes and had begun to list heavily to port. She had not been built to withstand that sort of punishment and her list increased steadily until, at 11:08, she rolled over and sank. The survivors from both ships were picked up and at 13:00 *Greif*, now a smoke-shrouded inferno, went down with her colours flying.

For the majority of the German surface fleet, however, morale had suffered severely from the long period of inactivity, and the opportunity now arose to improve this. That opportunity was a chance to provide support for an Irish republican rising in Dublin over the Easter period, the details of which were already known to the German authorities. Direct intervention was out of the question, but another raid on Yarmouth, with nearby Lowestoft and Zeppelin raids over southern England for good measure, would at least show the rebels that they did not lack support. In addition, it was felt that the raiders could complete their task before Beatty's battle cruisers could reach the area.

As usual, the German battle cruisers, commanded on this occasion by Rear Admiral Boedecker, would carry out a 30-minute bombardment while the High Seas Fleet under Admiral Scheer would cover their withdrawal. At noon on 24 April both groups, totalling 22 dreadnoughts and battle cruisers, five older battleships, 12 light cruisers, 48 destroyers and eight Zeppelins, set off for the English coast. Four hours later *Seydlitz* struck a mine. Her forward torpedo compartment was flooded and her speed fell away to 15 knots. Some time was lost transferring the admiral to *Lutzow*, largely because a report of torpedo tracks had resulted in ships moving out of what appeared to be a danger area. *Seydlitz* then returned home escorted by two destroyers and Zeppelin L7.

One of the most curious aspects of this operation is Scheer's fixation on Yarmouth and Lowestoft as his objective when, not all that far to the south was a far greater and more spectacular prize. This was an area known as The Downs, situated between Ramsgate and Dover, where, twice in every 24 hours, one hundred or more merchant ships waited for tidal conditions that would enable them to enter the river and reach the Port of London. The arrival of German battle cruisers and their escorts among them would have resulted in a massacre and provided Germany with an immense propaganda victory.

One officer who was fully aware of the threat was Commodore Tyrwhitt, commanding the 5th Light Cruiser Squadron, presently off the Suffolk coast. At first he was unsure of the precise enemy objective, but this became obvious when, at 03:50 Boedecker's four battle cruisers, six light cruisers and supporting destroyers were sighted, making for Lowestoft and Yarmouth. Tyrwhitt had only the light cruisers *Conquest, Cleopatra* and *Penelope* at his disposal, supported by two destroyer flotillas, so any sort of stand-up fight was out of the question. He took the only possible course of action by heading south in the hope that the enemy would pursue. The Germans, however, were temporarily distracted by the return of six Zeppelins that had abandoned their raid on London because of headwinds, poor visibility and strong opposition. Instead, bombs had been dropped in the areas of Norwich, Lincoln, Harwich and Ipswich, to little effect. L21 had caused some damage in Lowestoft at about 04:00 but had been pursued by three Bristol Scout aircraft based at the RNAS airfield at Yarmouth until it vanished into the clouds.

At about the same time the light cruiser *Rostock* spotted Tyrwhitt's ships to the south-west. For the moment, the light was too poor for accurate gunnery. At 04:10 the German battle cruisers opened a ten minute bombardment of Lowestoft, destroying or damaging over 200 civilian dwellings, fortunately without heavy loss of life, and then turned north to attack Yarmouth. Here the sighting of a British submarine in the act of diving caused sufficient alarm for Boedecker to turn south again after firing a shorter bombardment.

By 04:30 the light had improved sufficiently for the opposing cruisers to begin duelling ineffectively at 14,000 yards. At 04:45, however, the German battle cruisers arrived, opening a heavy and disturbingly accurate fire. *Conquest* was hit repeatedly, suffering 38 casualties of which 25 were fatal, but was able to maintain her speed. The destroyer *Laertes* was also hit and five of her crew were wounded. Having completed their mission, Boedecker's ships then turned away to rendezvous with the High Seas Fleet off Terschelling.

In Britain, the raid caused almost as much shock and anger as had the attacks on Scarborough, Whitby and the Hartlepools. In particular there was anger that, once again, the Royal Navy had not been able to act decisively. The Mayors of Lowestoft and Yarmouth lodged understandably vigorous protests that their towns should continue to receive regular visits from the Imperial German Navy and its Zeppelins. Fortunately, such was now the strength of the Grand Fleet that the Third Battle Squadron, reinforced by *Dreadnought* herself, was moved south to Sheerness on 2 May.

As for the Germans, they returned home with the satisfaction of having completed the task that they had set out to do at the cost of one repairable battle cruiser. They had also achieved some measure of revenge for an unfortunate incident that had taken place earlier in the year. During the course of the raid the light cruiser *Frankfurt* had sunk an armed patrol steamer and the destroyer *G-41* had sunk the armed trawler *King Stephen.* During the early hours of 2 February the *King Stephen* had been going about her normal civilian business. It was during the watch of her mate, George Denny, who saw distress rockets being fired some distance away. He roused the skipper, William Martin, who ordered the trawl to be brought in and secured while he laid off a course towards the signals. It took several hours to reach the area, where they found Zeppelin L19 in a sinking condition.

In a raging storm rain had battered the enormous envelope, increasing its weight so that it was unable to cope with high winds and had been driven down to sea level. The gondolas were already submerged and the huge hull was obviously filling with water and sinking. Seated on the half-submerged wreck were fourteen survivors. Martin discussed the situation with his eight-strong crew. The consensus of opinion was that some of the Germans were probably armed and that even if they all lacked weapons they heavily outnumbered the trawlermen and would almost certainly take over the vessel and sail her to Germany, where their saviours' reward would be a long spell in a prison camp. It was a horrible decision for a professional seaman to have to make. Had the

King Stephen been fitted with radio perhaps assistance could have been summoned, but she was not and in the circumstances Martin felt that he could only leave the Germans to their fate.

The authorities in Grimsby were not unsympathetic and decided that the matter should not be discussed publicly. Mate Denny, however, had other ideas and sold the story to a reporter from the *Grimsby Evening Mail*. Soon it had reached the national press. Copies of these editions reaching Germany through neutral countries generated understandable anger and demands for Martin to be punished. In fact, he was already a very sick man and died shortly after.

The *King Stephen* never sailed again as a fishing vessel. She was requisitioned and equipped as a Q ship. Commanded by a reserve officer, Lieutenant Tom Phillips, she had the misfortune to find herself under the guns of *G-41* during the bombardment of Yarmouth. Every German seaman knew the story of the *King Stephen* and Phillips' crew were roughly treated when they were taken aboard the enemy ship. It took a great deal of persuasion to convince their captors that an earlier crew had been responsible for abandoning those aboard the sinking Zeppelin. On reaching Germany they spent the rest of the war in Hameln prison camp. Phillips, however, was taken to Berlin for interrogation. Things would have gone badly for him until an English newspaper containing Martin's photograph was produced, convincing his captors that they had got the wrong man. So ended one of the most unfortunate incidents of the entire war at sea.

CHAPTER 9

Strafing the Island (1)

Count Ferdinand von Zeppelin was born in 1838. He served in the Royal Wurttemberg Army, in which he fought during the Franco-German War of 1870. In 1890 he left the Army feeling, as did many South German noblemen, that Prussia had far too much influence in the recently created German Empire. He then devoted himself to the development of the rigid dirigible airship which has born his name ever since. In fact, his organisation, the Luftshiffbau Zeppelin was not alone in manufacturing this type of airship, the Luftshiffbau Schutte-Lanz being a competitor during the early years, although by custom ever since every rigid airship has become known as a Zeppelin, just as vacuum cleaners are known as Hoovers and raincoats as Macintoshes.

Zeppelin chose hydrogen as the lifting agent for his airships, despite the terrible danger of fire, the outbreak of which was almost always fatal to the ships. The hydrogen was contained within huge gasbags along the interior of the hull, with provision for venting and water ballast tanks used to maintain stability while ascending or descending. These were contained in a long, sausage-shaped hull based on a complex internal girder construction surrounded by a flexible skin. Control and communications gondolas were suspended below, as were the ship's engines, the number of which varied according to type.

At first, Zeppelin's organisation was not a financial success and it was not until 1911 that his airline, the Deutsche Luftschiffahrts AG began to show that large numbers of passengers could be carried at a profit. This aroused the interest of the Imperial German Army and Navy. The obvious advantages were that the Zeppelin had a very long in-flight endurance which made it capable of long-range reconnaissance and, of course, it could also be armed with bombs for dropping on specific targets. Of the dis-advantages, fire has already been mentioned. In addition, the girder construction was so flimsy that clumsy handling in a shed or high winds on take-off or landing could wreck a ship. Even more serious was the fact that Zeppelins were extremely difficult to navigate. Even modest winds were capable of pushing the huge, lighter-than-air hulls many miles off course, while cloud cover could make it impossible to obtain a fix on the ground below. Later, a small car containing one or two observers and a telephone could be lowered by electric winch through the cloud and provide a view of the ground below, but the idea was not a success.

During World War One, Zeppelins served in every German theatre of war save East Africa, and even there one tried to get through, albeit unsuccessfully, by overflying Egypt and the Sudan. The Army preferred to use them for deep reconnaissance but would occasionally mount a bombing mission. The Navy used them as scouts for the operations of the High Seas Fleet but also carried out raids well inland into England, proving that nowhere was safe from the attentions of the Imperial Navy. Naval Zeppelin bases were established near Cuxhaven, at Ahlhorn near Oldenburg, Wittmundshaven (East Friesland), Tondern (Schlewig-Holstein, now Denmark) and, for a while, Hage, south of Nordeny. From these their route took them on a south-westerly course from which they would cross the North Sea to the East Anglian coast, from which the glow of

London's lights provided a distant beacon to steer by. Having carried out their mission, they would leave England by crossing the Kent coast and then head north-east to home.

Huge though the Zeppelins were, they generated very little awe in the professional flying community. In 1914 Royal Naval Air Service and Royal Flying Corps squadrons had been posted to the French and Belgian coast as a defence against German air operations in the Channel. On 8 October, flying a Sopwith Tabloid, Lieutenant R.G.L.Marix located a Zeppelin shed at Dusseldorf and dropped four 20-lb bombs onto it from a height of 600 feet. The resulting explosions were quickly followed by a roaring inferno, the flames of which reached as high as 500 feet, signifying the end of an Army Zeppelin, Z-9. Although the Tabloid received some damage from enemy fire, Marix managed to nurse it back to within 20 miles of Antwerp, completing the journey home on a borrowed bicycle. The following day the Allies withdrew from the city.

On 21 November an even more ambitious RNAS raid with three Avro 504bs was mounted from Belfort in Alsace against the birthplace of the Zeppelin, Friedrichshafen on Lake Constance. One airship was wrecked and considerable damage was done to the hangars and other facilities of this airship holy-of-holies. One aircraft was shot down, its pilot being seriously injured when he was attacked by a civilian mob. In contrast, the German military treated him with respect and great kindness while he was recovering in hospital.

On Christmas Day 1914 further incidents demonstrated how the naval air war was likely to develop. A squadron of light cruisers under the command of Commodore R.Y. Tyrwhitt escorted three specially converted Channel ferries, *Engadine*, *Riviera* and *Empress*, across the North Sea to a position close to the mouth of the Elbe, from which an attack could be made on the Zeppelin sheds at Cuxhaven. Nine Short floatplanes were lowered into the sea, of which only seven managed to lift off. The remainder flew to Cuxhaven where, although they were unable to identify the sheds, their appearance caused uproar. As the High Seas Fleet relied on Zeppelins for much of its reconnaissance, the risk of future raids was only too real. Furthermore, the German high command was seriously unsettled by the fact that so much valuable information on the fleet's disposition had been gathered by the British pilots that a number of warships were moved immediately. Amid the hullabaloo, the battle cruiser *Von der Tann* was involved in a collision and so seriously damaged that she had to be docked. Three of the floatplanes returned safely to their carriers. The pilots of three more were picked up by the submarine *E11*, and the last became a passenger aboard a Dutch fishing boat.

Meanwhile, a counter-attack had been launched on Tyrwhitt's cruisers by two Zeppelins, *L5* and *L6*, plus a number of seaplanes. None were hit, although some were near-missed and finally the German aircraft droned off. *L6*, with her crew frantically slapping patches on 600 bullet holes hissing hydrogen out of her gasbags, was very lucky to get home.

It is, of course, impossible to describe all the raids that took place over four years in a single chapter. Naturally, the Kaiser insisted in regulating what was going on and insisted that London was not to be attacked west of the Tower. This ruled out most of the best targets, including the City. The Imperial Chancellor, Theobald Bethmann-Holweg gave permission for the City to be attacked at weekends, when it was empty. It was then pointed out that it emptied every night, so that restriction was removed.

Finally, the Kaiser permitted attacks throughout the capital, with the exception of historic buildings and royal palaces. Nature imposed her own limitations when Zeppelin operations were restricted to the moonless half of the month. The first attack on the United Kingdom took place on 19/20 January 1915 and caused very little damage. In all, 42 raids were launched during the year with a variable number of airships, the first strategic air offensive aimed at the United Kingdom, with very mixed results, including the needless destruction of a large number of glasshouses at Cheshunt.

London was not attacked until 31 May, when seven people were killed and 38 wounded. On 6 June *L13*, commanded by Lieutenant Commander Heinrich Mathy, a brilliant navigator and the nearest thing to a Zeppelin ace, attacked Hull, causing £45,000 of damage. A riot ensued in which property believed to be in German ownership was wrecked. It was not just that fear was getting the better of people; they were angry, too, that the powers that be were apparently failing to provide them with adequate protection and several Royal Flying Corps personnel were roughed-up because of it. This was not justified, because the threat was being taken very seriously and a great deal was already being done, although it would be some time before a fully integrated defence system became operational.

On 8 September, Mathy was back in *L13*, carrying a two-ton bomb-load, including one of the new 660-lb bombs specially designed for use against England. This time his target was the City, in which he started extensive fires and destroyed buildings in the area north of St Paul's Cathedral. Anti-aircraft fire forced him to climb hurriedly to 11,200 feet, but his last bombs was used to damage the railway track leaving Broad Street Station and to destroy two motor buses. On this occasion he had caused over £500,000 worth of damage, killed 22 people and injured 87 more. Such was public anger that on 12 September the Admiralty appointed Admiral Sir Percy Scott, a gunnery expert of note, to command London's anti-aircraft defences.

One of the most remarkable raids of all took place on the night of 13/14 October, involving *L15* under the command of Lieutenant Commander Jaochim Breihaupt, another excellent navigator. Breihaupt penetrated central London and, flying steadily from west to east to the north of The Strand, dropped his bombs on Exeter Street, Wellington Street, Catherine Street, Aldwych, the Royal Courts of Justice, Carey

Street, Lincoln's Inn, Hatton Garden and Farringdon Road before heading for home. Behind lay a trail of death and destruction, including 28 killed and 60 injured. The number of casualties could have been higher as Breihaupt's course took him close by the capital's theatre land, where places of entertainment were packed to the doors. While leaving the target area, Breihaupt was also forced to climb sharply to avoid anti-aircraft fire, and noted with alarm that several aircraft were searching for him at a lower level, proof that the defence was stiffening.

Breihaupt's attack may have unsettled some Londoners, but in certain circles it was simply not done to acknowledge the fact. At the height of the attack, about 22:30, Mrs Patrick Campbell, the *doyenne* of the London stage and leading member of British society, was being fitted with a dress. She was leaning out of her window, trying to discover the cause of all the fuss, with two seamstresses hanging onto her bottom for dear life. 'They're bombing Derry and Thoms!' she announced in total disbelief. Obviously, the attempted destruction of one's favourite fashion house was taking things beyond acceptable limits.

During this period, unless luck was on their side, aircraft were at a disadvantage when engaging Zeppelins, for not only were they unable to match the airships' ability to gain altitude rapidly, their machine gun ammunition was unable to do more than puncture the gasbags inside the hull, damage which could be repaired quickly by a trained crew. An alternative was to drop bombs on the airship from above, but that was a very hit and miss affair, even if the necessary height could be gained. However, on the night on 6/7 June 1915 Sub-Lieutenant R.A.J. Warneford, piloting a tiny Morane, was on his way to bomb the Zeppelin sheds at Berchem Ste Agathe when he spotted *LZ-37* over Ostend. He closed in to attack but was not only driven off by machine gun fire, but also chased by the monster for a while. Without losing sight of the airship, he put his machine into a slow, steady climb until he reached the height of 11,000 feet.

Turning off his engine, he glided noiselessly down on *LZ-37*, 4,000 feet below, and, flying along the back of his opponent, dropped six 20-lb bombs onto it. Some must have detonated on the airship's hard internal skeleton, for there was a huge explosion that blew the little Morane upside down and caused some internal damage to the engine. Having recovered control of his machine, Warneford could see the flaming mass hurtling earthwards. It smashed into a convent, the only survivor being a quartermaster named Alfred Muhler who was thrown out of the control gondola when it crashed through a roof, landing on a bed bruised and singed but alive. For his part, Warneford managed to land his aircraft in enemy territory, where he was able to repair the damage and return home. His exploit won him the Victoria Cross but his story had a sad ending for, ten days later, he was killed in a flying accident.

In 1916 the number of Zeppelin raids mounted against 'the island,' as the crews termed the United Kingdom, increased three-fold, although the results achieved were far from commensurate with the additional effort involved. The principal reason for this was that the anti-aircraft defences of London and the Home Counties had improved beyond recognition. New and improved anti-aircraft guns were deployed throughout the capital and suburbs and in a secondary ring in the outlying hinterland, leaving a corridor in which British fighter aircraft could operate against the raiders without the risk of being hit by the anti-aircraft batteries. These were supplemented by searchlights and barrage balloons between which cable aprons were stretched, forcing the attackers to climb and therefore lose accuracy. These defences were duplicated to a lesser degree around the Thames estuary, the Kent and Essex coasts and further north along the east coast. In addition, the Royal Navy stationed guard ships along the Zeppelins' most likely avenues of approach, armed with anti-aircraft weapons. Special machine gun ammunition was also added to the fighters' armament, including Brock incendiary rounds, developed by the firework company of the same name, and Pomeroy explosive rounds. These were mixed together in the drum magazines of the Lewis guns that armed the anti-airship fighters.

In August 1916 Admiral Reinhard Scheer received a letter from Captain Peter Strasser, the energetic operational commander of the Imperial Navy's airship arm, promising him that his Zeppelins would inflict such serious damage on British civilian morale and economic life that their recovery was unlikely. It was indeed true that much larger, improved airships with the capacity to climb higher were being introduced, and that raids were now being carried out by groups of Zeppelins rather than by individual ships. However, the old problem of faulty navigation persisted, with commanders returning home convinced that their bombs had hit their target when they had actually landed many miles away. Again, the standard airship engine was a veritable minefield of trouble, causing numerous sorties to be aborted and contributing to the loss of ships. In the circumstances, it was an unwise prediction, especially as the British defence was beginning to take a steady toll.

On the night of 2/3 September no fewer than twelve naval airships, joined by four army craft flying from the Rhineland, set out for London. Among the latter was a new Schutte-Lanz craft, *SL-11*, commanded by a Captain Schramm. Approaching London from the north, *SL-11* was brilliantly illuminated by searchlights and surrounded by bursting anti-aircraft shells. Schramm decided to turn away, but three night fighters were already converging on him. Closest was Second Lieutenant William Leefe Robinson, who laced the huge hull with two drums of incendiary and explosive ammunition, without result. He then concentrated the fire of a third drum against one point near the tail. A glow appeared inside the envelope, grew in intensity and suddenly burst through in a roaring tongue of flame that briefly lit up another airship, *L-16*, over a mile distant. Then, stern first, *SL-11* crashed to earth near Cuffley in Essex, her wooden Schutte-Lanz skeleton continuing to burn long after the impact. There were no survivors. Robinson was awarded the Victoria Cross.

Simultaneously, after a good run in which serious ground fires had been started, *L-33*, one of the new 'super-Zeppelins,' sustained heavy damage from anti-aircraft fire and was crippled by a night fighter flown by Second Lieutenant Albert de Bathe Brandon. Her crew managed to land her near Little Wigborough, then set her on fire before marching towards the coast in the vain hope of finding a boat.

Mathy, now commanding *L-31*, took part in an eleven-strong raid on London during the night of 1 October. Having dropped his bombs, Mathy found himself under attack by four night fighters, one of which, piloted by Second Lieutenant Wulstan J. Tempest, came in from above and set the ship ablaze. The wreckage hit the ground at Potters Bar. Somehow, Mathy managed to jump clear but died from his injuries almost immediately. His loss was keenly felt throughout the airship service.

It was two months before naval Zeppelins appeared again in British skies. They avoided London because of its heavy defences, and attacked the North and Midlands instead. The raids were not a success and cost two Zeppelins shot down in flames; *L-34* over West Hartlepool and *L-21* off Lowestoft, having raided as far west as Newcastle-under Lyme.

For Count Zeppelin the airship was not the war-winning weapon he had hoped it would be. Zeppelin raids against the United Kingdom tailed away to 30 in 1917 and ten in 1918. Scheer's memoirs record the final days of the airship service.

A painful set-back occurred in January 1918 when, owing to the spontaneous combustion of one of the airships in Ahlhorn, the fire spread by the explosion spread to the remaining sheds, so that four Zeppelins and one Schutte-Lanz machine were destroyed. All the sheds, too, were rendered useless. After this, the fleet had, for the time being, only nine airships at its disposal.

That was not quite the end of the of the Zeppelin story. The Royal Navy had been developing the concept of the aircraft carrier for some time and had finally produced a workable design by converting the light battle cruiser *Furious* and fitting her with a flight deck. On 19 July 1918 she flew off six Sopwith Camels which mounted a successful attack on the airship base at Tondern, destroying Zeppelins *L-54* and *L-60*.

On 5 August five Zeppelins, led by Captain Strasser himself in the recently delivered *L-70*, mounted a final attack. *L-70* was attacked by de Havilland DH-4 fighters. Explosive ammunition blew a hole in the outer skin of the ship's stern. Within seconds flames spread rapidly along her length and the blazing wreckage tumbled seawards from a height of some 15,000 feet. The British pilots were horrified to watch the entire airship consume itself in less than a minute. There were no survivors. Strasser was a well-liked commander who had often accompanied his crews on their missions and had never lost faith in the airship concept.

Six days later Zeppelin *L-53* was carrying out a reconnaissance patrol over the North Sea. No doubt the crew noticed, far below, a destroyer travelling at speed. It did not attract a great deal of interest as the airship was well beyond the range of its guns. For some unexplained reason it seemed to be towing a lighter, although the details were unclear. Had *L-53* been flying lower she would have seen one of the strangest anti-aircraft systems ever devised, for on the lighter was a Sopwith Camel. The wind created by the speed of the destroyer's passage created just enough lift for the biplane to become airborne. It took an hour before the Camel could reach a height at which the airship could be engaged. At a range of 100 yards, drum after drum was emptied into the Zeppelin's belly, sending it into a fiery death-dive.

HMS *Tiger* in action at Jutland.

The 5th Battle Squadron at high speed in heavy seas.

Damage to Q turret on HMS *Lion* after Jutland.

A Krupp 12-inch shell that pierced HMS *Defender* during the battle.

Commander Loftus-Jones VC.

Flotilla leader destroyers *Broke* and *Swift* (in the background) formed part of the famous Dover Patrol and on 17 April 1917 were victorious in a hard-fought action against German destroyers off the Dutch coast.

Broke working up to her maximum speed of 32 knots. At Jutland she had sustained heavy casualties, which may explain the ferocity with which her crew repelled German boarders during the action mentioned above. Her captain on this occasion was Commander E.R.G.R. Evans, subsequently known as 'Evans of the *Broke*'. He had survived Scott's Second Antarctic Polar Expedition 1910–1913 which he commemorated with a toy penguin nailed to his foremast. He retired in 1936 as an admiral with the title 1st Baron Mountevans.

With *Broke*'s engines at full power, Evans drover her remorselessly into his opponent's hull, carving a huge gash from which she could not hope to recover. Hand-to-hand fighting is taking place on *Broke*'s forecastle. The odd black-and-white striped pennant was peculiar to the Imperial German Navy and was a recognition aid during night fighting. (*Royal Navy Museum*)

HMS *Broke*.

Zeebrugge. Charles De Lacy's painting shows the requisitioned Mersey ferry *Daffodil* pushing the old cruiser *Vindictive* hard against the mole while troops swarm ashore across the two surviving brows. Although the raid was only a partial success it raised the morale of the British public and damaged German belief in ultimate victory. Significantly, when those troops and naval personnel stationed along the Belgian coast were withdrawn they played a prominent part in the mutinies that destroyed Imperial Germany. *(IWM Pic. 1084)*

The crew of HMS *Mary Rose*.

The end of it all. On 21 November most of the High Seas Fleet, having landed its ammunition, torpedoes, breech blocks, gun sights and gun control equipment, sailed from its bases into internment under the guns of the Grand Fleet and its allies and the watchful eyes of non-rigid naval airships. In contrast to the fleet that had fought at Jutland, the German ships presented a dirty, unkempt appearance and the majority of their crews consisted of mutineers only too pleased that their discharge was imminent. Following a brief stop in the Firth of Forth, the High Seas Fleet made its final voyage to Scapa Flow where, in erroneous belief that they were to be surrendered to the Allies, its ships were scuttled by their crews. The photograph shows the battle cruiser squadron on 21 November with (left to right) *Seydlitz, Moltke, Hindenburgh* and *Derfflinger*. (*IWM Q.20614*)

This was the last enemy airship to be destroyed by British fighters during the war.

The huge size of the Zeppelins, caught in searchlight beams or sliding across a gap in the clouds, coupled with their ability to hover, produced widespread fear among the civilian population of Great Britain, generated by the knowledge that their island was no longer a safe haven from enemy activity, but it did not break their will to fight, as had been intended. Zeppelins killed 528 people and wounded 1,156 more. They also caused enormous damage, but it was spread across a very wide area. In addition, they tied down 17,340 men, hundreds of anti-aircraft guns, searchlights and barrage balloons, plus numerous RNAS and RFC squadrons, all of which could have been usefully employed in other theatres of war.

To crew a Zeppelin was to risk a particularly horrible death. About 1,100 Zeppelin crewmen lost their lives, the second highest proportion of those serving in any branch of the German armed services, the highest being U-boat crews. John Terraine provides some idea of the scale of Zeppelin losses in his book *White Heat – The New Warfare 1914–18*. He points out that of the 130 airships employed by the German Army and Navy during the war, only 15 existed when the Armistice was signed. Of the remainder, 31 were scrapped, seven were wrecked by bad weather, 38 were accidently damaged beyond economic repair, 39 were destroyed by enemy warships or land forces, while a further 17 fell victim to the RFC or RNAS, either in the air or as a result of bombing.

CHAPTER 10

A Battle Long Awaited – Jutland and Its Sequel

Admiral Reinhard Scheer, commander of the High Seas Fleet, seemed to enjoy a closer relationship with his sovereign than had either of his predecessors. He certainly possessed more drive and the success of the raids against Lowestoft and Scarborough, while modest, suggested that here was a commander who could produce results. His concept of grand strategy also exceeded theirs in that he was able to convince the Kaiser that continued naval raiding would erode the trust of the British population in the Royal Navy and that if, as originally envisaged, a significant portion of its strength could be eliminated, the spectre of invasion would so haunt London's politicians that many thousands of British troops, together with all their artillery, aircraft and equipment, would be withdrawn from the Western Front for the defence of the homeland. Thanks to the Zeppelin raids, thousands of men, anti-aircraft guns and fighter aircraft were already being held back in England rather than sent to France. In due course the Western Front would be so severely weakened that the French would request an armistice. This alone would justify further aggressive use of the High Seas

Fleet, coupled with continued air attacks, and warrant taking the obvious risks involved. As for Russia, her capacity to fight had all but been destroyed in two years of total war, and her collapse was simply a matter of time.

It might have been a German dream, but at Scapa Flow Admiral Sir John Jellicoe had already worked out the details for himself. A German defeat at sea would have no effect on the German armies' performance on land, whereas a British defeat would have a disastrous effect on Allied strategy. Winston Churchill, who had also evaluated the potential of the situation, perceptively described Jellicoe as 'the only man who could lose the war in an afternoon'. For that reason Beatty's Battle Cruiser Fleet had been strengthened by the addition of Rear Admiral Hugh Evan-Thomas's 5th Battle Squadron consisting of the fast battleships *Barham*, *Valiant*, *Warspite* and *Malaya*.

Scheer accepted the fact that every time the High Seas Fleet put to sea, Beatty seemed to be waiting, although he did not know why. His plan was to trap and destroy Beatty's ships by tempting them south with a bombardment of Sunderland, to be carried out by the German battle cruisers, once more under the command of Hipper. At this juncture the High Seas Fleet would pounce before Jellicoe's Grand Fleet could intervene and Germany would achieve an important naval victory. Early warning of the enemy's approach would be provided by a flight of scouting Zeppelins.

When the operation commenced on 31 May a haze covered the operational area. Despite this, Scheer decided to proceed without the Zeppelins. Hipper steered north and then north-west on a course that would avoid Dogger Bank and then take him directly to the objective, while Scheer followed with the High Seas Fleet, its battle squadrons in line ahead, on a more northerly heading. Both suspected that Beatty and Jellicoe were at sea but lacked any hard intelligence. In fact, Beatty and Evan-Thomas were already well on their way towards the intended battleground, and Jellicoe was pounding south from Scapa Flow with the

Grand Fleet's battleships deployed in six columns, ready to form line to port or starboard as the situation demanded.

At 15:00 Beatty and Hipper were still some distance apart when an entirely innocent event brought them together. Between the two fleets a Danish tramp steamer, the *F.J. Fjord*, was going about her lawful business. She was not in the best of health and her chief engineer distrusted the accuracy of her steam gauge. Tapping it, he saw the needle jump to the red sector. Reaching for the voice pipe, he informed the captain that it would be necessary to heave to and reduce

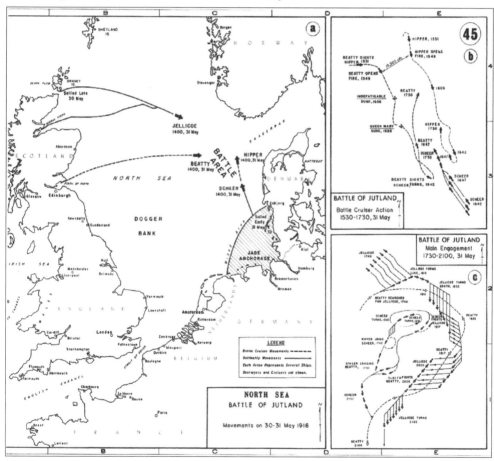

Map 5. The Battle of Jutland 30–31 May 1916.

pressure to safe levels. The captain agreed and the slow thump of the engine died away. With a shattering roar a continuous plume of steam leapt upwards from the funnel as the engineer opened the escape valve.

There was little wind to disperse it and cruisers and destroyers from both opposing screens closed in to investigate its source. Recognising each other, they opened fire at once. The Battle of Jutland, an encounter unique in the history of naval warfare, had begun. Clouds of funnel smoke identified the converging presence of both fleets, the respective commanders of which reached instinctive decisions. Hipper turned south with the intention of luring Beatty to destruction under the guns of the High Seas Fleet, while Beatty swung onto a parallel course, hoping to destroy his old enemy. Five German battle cruisers (*Lutzow, Derfflinger, Seydlitz, Moltke* and *Von der Tann*) were opposed by six British (*Lion, Princess Royal, Queen Mary, Tiger, New Zealand* and *Indefatigable*), although Beatty has been sharply criticised for not creating a decisive situation by waiting for Evan-Thomas's slightly slower dreadnoughts to catch up.

At 15:48 the battle cruisers of both sides opened fire, closing the range from 18,000 to 12,000 yards. Hipper had informed Scheer of the situation and the latter, presently some 60 miles to the south, was doing his best to close the gap quickly and complete Beatty's destruction. This was no easy matter as the speed of his fleet was limited to 18 knots, all that could be squeezed out of his pre-dreadnought battleship squadron. Simultaneously, Jellicoe's dreadnoughts were heading towards the scene of action at their best speed.

As the opposing lines of battle cruisers charged south, they passed either side of a barque, her sails hanging limp in the windless air. For the crew of the sailing ship, the experience must have been terrifying as hundreds of large calibre shells passed overhead in both directions with a sound like tearing cloth. There was no doubt that the German gunnery was the better. Aboard Beatty's *Lion*, Q (midships) turret was penetrated and most of its crew were killed.

Burning cordite charges would have flashed down into the magazine had not a mortally wounded Royal Marine Light Infantry officer, Major Francis Harvey, ordered the magazine doors to be closed and the compartment flooded. At 16:05 a shell exploded in *Indefatigable*'s A turret. The flash passed down the trunking into the magazine and the ship was simply blown apart in a huge column of smoke and flame. Of her entire crew, only two men survived. At 16:26 the *Queen Mary* shared a similar fate. By coincidence, for the second time in her history, one of *Seydlitz*'s turrets was penetrated by a shell that killed everyone within it. On this occasion, however, the repairs previously effected prevented the flash reaching the magazine and she survived.

By now, Evan-Thomas's dreadnoughts had caught up. Their gunnery was far batter than that of Beatty's battle cruisers and they soon began handing out a beating to Hipper's ships. Hipper, horrified by the damage that was being inflicted, turned away as soon as he sighted the leading ships of the High Seas Fleet at 17:00. The destroyer flotillas of both sides now surged forward to engage in a fast-moving *melee* in which the German *V27* and *V29* were sent to the bottom while a torpedo launched by *Petard* blew a huge hole in the side of *Seydlitz*. Some British destroyers even launched suicidal attacks on the leading dreadnoughts of Scheer's line. Of these, *Nestor* and *Nomad* went down fighting with their colours flying, the survivors of the former being chivalrously picked up by a German destroyer. In the meantime the light cruiser *Southampton* had pressed on to the south and radioed the position, course and strength of the High Seas Fleet. This priceless piece of intelligence was confirmed by Beatty, who reversed course at 17:26. The move was covered by Evan-Thomas's battleships who shot so well that they not only obtained hits on the leading dreadnoughts of Scheer's line, *Konig*, *Grosser*, *Kurfurst* and *Markgraf*, but also on Hipper's battle cruisers, which were now beginning to look increasingly battered. The tables had now been turned and it was Hipper and Scheer who, all unsuspecting, were sailing into a trap.

Jellicoe's columns deployed to port to form a line extending across the horizon, while the 3rd Battle Cruiser Squadron, consisting of *Invincible*, *Inflexible* and *Indomitable*, set off south to join Beatty. On sighting the Grand Fleet, Beatty swung eastwards to take up position at the head of the British line. At 18:15, emerging from the murk created by hundreds of smoke-belching funnels, Scheer and Hipper were horrified to discover that Jellicoe had crossed their T and that having been the hunters they had now become the hunted. Hipper was particularly taken aback by the fact that despite losing two of his battle cruisers, Beatty was now actually stronger than he had been at the start of the battle. In due course, his chagrin evidently communicated itself to the German official historian who described the Royal Navy as a hydra, referring to the mythical monster with so many heads that it did not matter how many one cut off. At 18:17 gunfire blazed the length of Jellicoe's line, blasting thousands of shells towards the German fleet. *Lutzow*, Hipper's flagship, became a battered, hopeless wreck. Hipper was forced to transfer his flag to a destroyer from which he watched his battle cruisers, the pride of the Imperial Navy and the favourite of the German public, progressively blown apart. All of *Von der Tann*'s turrets were put out of action; *Seydlitz* was awash from the bows with water slopping as far as her middle deck; *Derfflinger*, having received no less than twenty hits, was also down by the bows and had lost the ability to use her radio. Her commander, Captain Hartog, had temporarily assumed command of the battle cruisers in Hipper's absence, and this made his task doubly difficult.

In Scheer's line, *Konig*, hit time and again, was listing badly while *Markgraf*, with serious engine room damage, was forced to reduce speed. This was the last situation Scheer had hoped to find himself in, but as a sound professional he had allowed for it and exercised his ships in a manoeuvre known as the Battle Turn-Away in which each ship reversed course individually rather than turning in succession at the same point. By 18:35 he decided that his ships had taken more than enough punishment and he gave the signal. As the German fleet began to fade into the evening mist a final salvo from *Derfflinger* exploded aboard *Invincible*, which blew up from exactly the same cause as the earlier battle cruiser losses.

The fighting between the capital ships had been savage, but equally fierce duels were being fought between the cruisers and destroyers of both fleets. The light cruiser *Chester* unexpectedly found herself surrounded by an entire German light cruiser squadron consisting of the *Frankfurt*, *Wiesbaden*, *Pillau* and *Elbing*. Despite being hit repeatedly and sustaining heavy casualties among her crew, she succeeded in leading her opponents to within range of the British battle cruisers. The result was that a 12-inch shell exploded inside *Pillau*'s engine room, putting four boilers out of action and thereby turning her into a cripple, while *Frankfurt* limped off, seriously damaged. *Wiesbaden* was reduced to a blazing hulk but whatever chance her damage control parties might have had of saving her vanished when the destroyer *Onslow* and the armoured cruisers *Warrior* and *Defence* came upon her. Nevertheless, she continued to fight on as best she could until a torpedo finally sent her to the bottom. In response, *Defence* was seriously damaged by the fire of *Derfflinger* and no fewer than four German battleships. The destroyer *Shark* was smashed to burning wreckage by the fire of enemy cruisers and destroyers while leading a hopeless torpedo attack on the enemy's battle cruisers. Her captain, Commander Loftus Jones, having already lost his right leg and sustained further wounds to his face and thigh, ordered a White Ensign to be hoisted in place of that which had been shot away. One by one, *Shark*'s guns were silenced until only one, manned by three men, continued to spit defiance. The moment came when Loftus Jones recognised that she was going down by the bows and gave permission for the ship to be abandoned. Shortly after, she was given the *coup de grace* by two torpedoes. Loftus Jones was posthumously awarded the Victoria Cross and the six men of his crew who survived were given the Distinguished Service Medal.

Jellicoe could have pursued Scheer and doubtless sunk a number of German stragglers, but he wanted to inflict even greater damage on his opponents. Scheer had retreated westwards and it was obvious that sooner or later he would have to turn east to regain his bases. Jellicoe therefore set the Grand Fleet on a southerly course, confident that Scheer would have to cross this. This was exactly what happened. At 19:20 the High Seas Fleet again ran head-on into Jellicoe's line of battle and sustained a fearful pounding of which the battle cruisers received the major share. Aboard *Seydlitz* and *Derfflinger* damage control parties struggled to bring raging fires under control. *Von der Tann* was left with only one gun in action and a wrecked control tower but her captain gallantly remained in line hoping that his ship would draw fire intended for her consorts. *Lutzow*, crippled, fell further and further behind until, at 01:45, she was torpedoed by her own destroyer escort. Only *Moltke* retained some semblance of normality, enabling Hipper to board her later and assume control of his shattered command.

Thanks to their being silhouetted against the setting sun, the Germans had much the worst of this exchange of fire, while their opponents, hardly visible against the darkening sky to the east suffered little. Scheer stuck it for about five minutes, during which his dreadnoughts *Markgraf*, *Grosser Kurfurst* and *Konig* all received further punishment while *Helgoland*, lying fourth in his battle line, was hit by a 15-inch shell that wrecked a 5.9-inch gun and punched a huge hole in the hull through which some 80 tons of water flooded into the ship . Close to hysteria, he ordered another Battle Turn-Away while the remaining battle cruisers covered the manoeuvre by charging the British line. This would have achieved very little and almost certainly have resulted in heavy if not terminal loss for those involved. Nevertheless, from such seeds do legends grow. It was said, and became an article of faith in the German Navy, that he had ordered the battle cruisers to 'close the enemy and ram!' His actual words were, *'Grosser Kreuzer, Gefechtswendung rein in den Fiend! Ran!'* (Battle cruisers, turn toward the enemy and engage him closely! At him!) Obediently, the four battle cruisers that could, commenced their attack, surging through a torrent of exploding shells. Minutes later, Scheer recovered his composure and cancelled the order, leaving his destroyers to mount a mass torpedo attack.

In such circumstances, the defence was to turn towards or away from the running torpedoes, allowing them to pass harmlessly between ships. Jellicoe chose to turn away, giving an added margin of safety by letting the torpedoes run to the point that their fuel was exhausted. Not one torpedo found its mark, while six German destroyers were damaged and a seventh, *S35*, was sunk. There were those who, with the benefit of hindsight, criticised Jellicoe for not turning *towards* the torpedoes, as this would have meant that the enemy remained within range and in view. Against this, he had no wish to let Scheer claim serious damage to or sinking of several British dreadnoughts. It was unfortunate that contact was temporarily lost but both fleets were now running south on parallel courses and it seemed quite probable that it would be regained. At 20:20, with the last of the light fading rapidly, there was a brief engagement between the battle cruisers and the German pre-dreadnoughts, leading Scheer's line since the last Battle Turn-Away which were sent to assist but were forced to retreat when hits were scored on the battleships *Schleswig-Holstein* and *Pommern* as well as on the cruiser *Stettin*.

Scheer had no wish to renew the battle and, aware that first light would appear at about 03:30, he knew that he could not delay turning south-eastwards any longer, even if it meant fighting his way through Jellicoe's line. This time, luck was on his side, for Jellicoe's fleet was several knots faster than his own so that when he gave the order to change course at 21:30 he broke through the light units covering the rear of the British line. A series of confused actions followed in which the Germans had a slight advantage in that they had laid greater emphasis of training for night fighting, including the use of starshells and searchlights. The British lost several destroyers, the armoured cruiser *Black Prince* and the light cruiser *Tipperary*. In addition, the cruisers *Southampton* and *Dublin* sustained serious damage. The German cruisers *Frauenlob* and *Rostock* were torpedoed and sunk. The cruiser *Elbing* was also hit by a torpedo. Whatever chance she had of survival was snuffed out when she was rammed by one of her own dreadnoughts, the *Posen*, and finally abandoned to sink. The destroyer *Obedient* slammed a torpedo into the pre-dreadnought *Pommern*, which blew up and sank. During the early hours of 1 June the High Seas Fleet passed the Horns Reef, marking the 120-mile swept channel leading to its anchorages. At 05:20 the dreadnought *Ostfriesland* struck a British mine laid the previous night but managed to limp into harbour. Had the return voyage been just a few miles longer *Seydlitz*, almost hidden by belching clouds of dense black smoke, drawing 42 feet of water at the bows and with hundreds of tons of water aboard, would never have reached home. As it was, she grounded several times and finally had to be towed into harbour stern-first. The British remained off the Horns Reef until 11:00 on 1 June, then turned for home in rising seas that claimed the *Warrior*, badly damaged and under tow.

So ended the Battle of Jutland, known, as Skagerrak in Germany. When the final accounting was done, the Grand Fleet's losses amounted to three battle cruisers, three armoured cruisers and eight destroyers, a total of fourteen ships. The High Seas Fleet lost one pre-dreadnought battle-ship, one battle cruiser, four light cruisers, and five destroyers a total of eleven ships. British casualties amounted to 6,097 killed, about half of whom were lost in the three battle cruisers, and 510 wounded; the Germans lost 2,551 killed and 507 wounded.

On the basis of statistics and the fact that Scheer had brought his fleet home, the German press claimed a stunning victory. Scheer and Hipper both received Germany's highest military decoration, the *Pour le Merite*. Scheer declined to accept a title but the King of Bavaria granted Hipper a knighthood and with it the right to add 'von' to his name; knowing the truth of the matter, he was not terribly interested in either. An unexpectedly large number of lesser mortals received the Iron Cross.

Across the North Sea news spread among the British public that a major fleet action had taken place. It was confidently expected that the Royal Navy had won a second Trafalgar and, indeed, it was felt to be nothing less than an entitlement. However, the Admiralty's first official communiqué on the subject, issued on the morning of 3 June, produced such a sense of shock that it was widely remembered over thirty years later.

On the afternoon of Wednesday May 31, a naval engagement took place off the coast of Jutland. The British ships on which the brunt of the fighting fell were the Battle Cruiser Fleet and some cruiser and light cruisers supported by four fast battleships. Among these the losses were heavy. The German battle fleet, aided by low visibility, avoided prolonged action with our main forces, and soon after these appeared on the scene the enemy returned to port, though not before receiving severe damage from our battleships. The battle cruisers *Queen Mary*, *Indefatigable*, *Invincible* and the cruisers *Defence* and *Black Prince* were sunk. The *Warrior* was disabled and after being towed for some time, had to be abandoned by her crew. It is also known that the destroyers *Tipperary*, *Turbulent*, *Fortune*, *Sparrowhawk* and *Ardent* were lost and six others are not yet accounted for. No British battleships or light cruisers were sunk. The enemy's losses are serious. At least one battle cruiser was destroyed; one battleship reported sunk by our destroyers during a night attack; two cruisers were disabled and probably sunk. The exact number of enemy destroyers disposed of during the action cannot be ascertained with any certainty, but it must have been large.

Traditionally, the Royal Navy was a reticent service that shied away from triumphalism, but the tone of the Admiralty's communiqué and its successor were so negative – to say nothing of being incomplete and inaccurate – that it might have been reporting a serious defeat. Jellicoe was furious, yet despite his fully justified protests, the Admiralty studiously avoided using the word 'victory' and, reasoned many, if there had not been a British victory, there must have been a British defeat. It was a message from King George himself that placed the matter in its correct perspective:

I regret that the German High Seas Fleet, in spite of its heavy losses, was enabled by the misty weather to evade the full consequences of an encounter they have always professed to desire but for which, when the opportunity arrived, they showed no inclination.

The neutrals tended to agree. Indeed, Jutland could be seen as yet another escape story. At its simplest, Sheer had gone to sea and Jellicoe had chased him back into harbour. Not one cargo of war material or foodstuffs to feed an increasingly hungry population reached Germany as a direct result of Jutland. Nothing had changed and the Royal Navy's blockade continued to strangle Imperial Germany.

Once the euphoria had subsided, there were plenty of level headed Germans able to see beyond the simple statistics of loss. Those who watched their shattered ships make their painful way into harbour saw nothing to celebrate. Among them was Scheer, who had received so many plaudits and now recognised that a limit had been reached. His view was that the High Seas Fleet must never again fight such a

battle, even if the respective losses were in the same proportion. In his opinion, it was simply not possible to defeat
the Royal Navy in a surface engagement. The accuracy of
this prediction was confirmed when, during the evening
of 2 June, Jellicoe, despite having to dock several ships,
was able to report the Grand Fleet ready for action at four
hours' notice. Scheer, on the other hand, indicated that
the High Seas Fleet would not be ready until the middle
of August, and even then *Seydlitz* and *Derfflinger* would not
complete their repairs until, respectively, September and
October. Somehow, he managed to convince the Kaiser
that the surface fleet's real value lay in absorbing so much
of Great Britain material and manpower resources, rather
than as a theoretical bargaining counter in any future peace
negotiations.

There was, however, one task that he must perform.
His men had understandably been shaken by the enemy's
murderous gunfire, the destruction caused by high explosive
shells, and the horrible shrieks of comrades torn apart. They
knew that they had hit the enemy hard, but it was they who
had been forced to seek refuge in harbour. In the circumstances, they found the jubilation of the civilians, who had
no idea what had actually taken place, somewhat over-
drawn. As a good commander, Scheer knew that he must
restore their morale. His attempt to bombard Sunderland
had been rudely interrupted by Beatty and Jellicoe. Now, he
would repeat it, with adequate Zeppelin reconnaissance to
warn him of their approach.

On 18 August he put to sea with the two remaining battle
cruisers, 18 battleships and, to prevent his being surprised
as he had on the last occasion, a scouting force of Zeppelins
would provide advance reconnaissance over a wide area. As
usual, Room 40 had provided advance warning of the High
Seas Fleet's assembly. Not only were Beatty and Jellicoe at
sea in overwhelming strength, the Harwich Force had also
been ordered out. This was spotted by Zeppelin *L13* and
reported by radio as including a squadron of battleships. It

was also, the report continued, within striking distance of Scheer to the south. Delighted, Scheer changed course in pursuit only to discover that his quarry consisted of smaller warships. It was now too late for him to carry out his original intention of bombarding Sunderland and he turned for home. By then, the distance between Jellicoe and Scheer was too great for an engagement to take place. The only losses incurred during the day were the light cruisers *Nottingham* and *Falmouth*, torpedoed and sunk by U-boats, and the dreadnought *Westfalen* damaged by a British submarine. On 18 October Scheer initiated another sortie but cancelled it and returned to harbour when a British submarine torpedoed the light cruiser *Munchen* in the Heligoland Bight. Thereafter, save for individual ships, the heavy units of the High Seas Fleet spent the rest of the war in harbour, their best officers and men transferring to the U-boat service while the morale of the remainder began to rot.

CHAPTER 11

Strafing the Island (2)

As the Zeppelin offensive against the United Kingdom began to lose its momentum, the High Command of the German armed forces decided to attach greater importance to the operations of the Imperial German Air Service. General Ernst von Hoeppner was appointed commander of this vastly expanded arm, with Colonel Hermann Thomsen as his Chief of Staff. From the outset, Hoeppner was more aggressive in his choice of primary targets, which would include the Houses of Parliamernt, Whitehall, Downing Street, the Admiralty, the War Office, the Bank of England and the newspaper production district of Fleet Street, the intention being to prove that no one in the British political, armed forces, financial or press establishments should feel any safer than the average citizen. Some raids would be delivered in daylight, the result being to further damage British morale.

As luck would have it, a suitable unit was stationed near Ostend on the Belgian coast, oddly named for security reasons as the *Ostend Brieftauben Abteiling*, that is, the Ostend Carrier Pigeon Battalion. This was to be equipped with Gotha heavy bombers, which had already entered production, and the Giant super bomber, which was approaching its production phase. The twin-engined Gotha bi-planes were considered to be huge in their day and could initially reach a height of 15,000 feet, which was well beyond the capacity of contemporary British fighters. With a maximum speed of 87 mph, they possessed a range of 500 miles and were capable of carrying a bomb load of 1,100-lbs. Defensive armament consisted of two machine guns. Depending upon mark, the Giants were powered by two to five engines and could also reach a height of 15,000 feet and had a maximum speed of approximately 85 mph. In addition to carrying a respectable bomb load, they possessed a formidable defensive armament of nose, dorsal, ventral and two upper wing machine guns.

Officially, the 'Ostend Carrier Pigeons,' commanded by Captain Ernst Brandenburger, were known as the *England-geschwerder*, or England Squadron. Nominally, this was sub-divided into six flights each of six aircraft. Hoeppner's view was that a small, specialist bomber unit such as this could achieve far better results than the Zeppelins. He pointed out, for example, that 18 Gothas carrying the same bomb load as three Zeppelins, were capable of arriving over London simultaneously, a feat never achieved by three Zeppelins, and thus represented far better value for money. The activities of the *Englandgeschwerder* were given the codename of Operation Turk's Cross.

At first glance, Hoeppner's ideas were entirely reasonable. There were, however, several factors that he had failed to take into account. The route of the raiders, having crossed the North Sea, was entirely predictable. They would overfly Essex to reach London then, having dropped their bombs, would turn left and leave England via the Kent coast. This meant that they would not only face the dense anti-aircraft belt already set up to counter the Zeppelin raids, but also be vulnerable to interception by the RFC and RNAS fighter squadrons based around Dunkirk. Again, their operational radius was far shorter than that of the Zeppelins, so that their potential target area was limited to London and a small segment of south-eastern England, leaving the rest of the

country virtually untroubled. Furthermore, the civil population had become accustomed to air attacks and learned
to live with them. Again, while there was something faintly
other-worldly about Zeppelins, biplanes were familiar sights,
even if these were far larger than usual. The element of
shock had been replaced by stoicism.

The first Gotha raid, involving 21 aircraft, took place
against Folkstone and Shorncliffe Camp on 25 May 1917.
Ninety-five people were killed and 195 were injured, while
damage caused was valued at £19,405. One Gotha was lost
over the English Channel, precise cause unknown, while
another crashed on landing. The second raid, by 22 Gothas,
against Sheerness and Shoeburyness, took place on 5 June
but produced disappointing results at the cost of one aircraft shot down. On 13 June the *Englandgeschwerder*'s third
raid, involving 18 Gothas, was directed at London and
Margate, killed 162, injured 432 and caused £129,498 worth
of damage as well as one British aircraft forced down. And
so it continued with several raids per month by day or night,
reaching a maximum number of seven raids in September
1917, then trailing away to end in May 1918. The results
achieved were mixed, varying between £238,816 worth
of damage inflicted during a night raid on London and
Margate on 18/19 December 1917 to just £129 on the night of
28/29 September when 23 Gothas and two Giants struck
at London and the coasts of Suffolk, Essex and Kent. This
attack was something of a disaster for the *Englandgeschwerder*
as only three Gothas and the Giants reached their respective
target areas. Three Gothas were shot down and six more
crashed on landing, the cost being just one British fighter
damaged on landing. This was also the first occasion on
which the Giants were committed to action.

The following list of German losses gives some idea of
how efficient the British air defences had become:

25 May 1917	1 Gotha lost, 1 crash landed
5 June 1917	1 Gotha shot down

7 July 1917	1 Gotha shot down, 4 crash landed on return
22 July	1 Gotha crash landed on return
12 August 1917	1 Gotha shot down, 4 crashed on landing
22 August 1917	3 Gothas shot down
4/5 September 1917	1 Gotha missing
25/25 September 1917	1 Gotha crashed on return
25/26 September 1917	1 Gotha missing
28/29 September 1917	3 Gothas shot down, 6 crashed on landing
29/30 September 1917	1 Gotha shot down, 1 forced down in neutral Holland
31 October/ 1 November 1917	5 Gothas crashed on landing
5/6 December 1917	5 Gothas crashed on landing
18/19 December 1917	2 Gothas shot down by AA fire, 1 missing, 1 crashed on landing
28/29 January 1918	1 Gotha shot down, 1 crashed on landing
7/8 March 1918	2 Giants crash landed on return
19/20 May 1918	1 Gotha forced down over England, 5 shot down, 1 crashed on return journey

The last raid listed above was a night attack directed at London, Faversham and Dover. As planned, it involved 38 Gothas, three Giants and two reconnaissance aircraft, but only 28 of the Gothas, the Giants and the reconnaissance aircraft reached their targets. The raid was something of a swan song in every sense of the word. Indeed, despite all the casualties caused and the damage inflicted, as a strategic offensive the operations carried out by the heavy bombers had been no more successful than those of the Zeppelins.

During the last months of the war, responsibility for air attacks on the United Kingdom was handed back to the Navy's Zeppelins which, as described in the last chapter, were only capable of conducting a kind of broken-backed warfare that achieved nothing.

A generation later, many of the lessons learned defending the United Kingdom against attack by Count Zeppelin's airships and General Hoeppner's heavy bombers were put to good use against Hitler's Luftwaffe.

CHAPTER 12

North and South – Destroyer Actions, Attacks on Scandinavian Convoys, Second Battle of Heligoland Bight

In the aftermath of Jutland and Scheer's abortive foray in August 1916, a calm descended upon the central area of the North Sea. In one way this may have seemed curious as this was the very fulcrum of the naval war, yet in others it was entirely reasonable. Jellicoe, for example, was not only aware of technical shortcomings in some of the Grand Fleet's ships, notably the battle cruisers, but was also wary of potential traps posed by the enemy's mines and U-boats. He therefore decided that his ships would not proceed further south than 55° 30'. For his part, Scheer knew that he dared not risk the High Seas Fleet in another general action. The result was that, for the first time in the war, both sides possessed numerous destroyers that had previously been tied down escorting the capital ships.

There were only two exits to the Atlantic from the North Sea. One, in the north, lay between Scotland and Norway and was not only patrolled incessantly but was also adjacent to the Grand Fleet's anchorage at Scapa Flow. The second, in the south, was the Straits of Dover. Control of this was absolutely vital because of the constant passage of troops and supplies across the English Channel from southern English ports to France. Two naval forces had been established in the war's early days to provide security. The larger of the two was Commodore Reginald Tyrwhitt's Harwich Force, which in 1916 consisted of the 5th Cruiser Squadron's five ships, plus the 9th and 10th Destroyer Flotillas with 36 destroyers and four flotilla leaders or light cruisers. As we have seen, the Harwich Force frequently had responsibilities in the North Sea, and was usually unable to detach more than one flotilla for operations in the Straits. The principal burden of responsibility for the Straits rested with the Dover Patrol, commanded by Vice Admiral Sir Francis Bacon. This consisted of two light cruisers or flotilla leaders, 24 destroyers, eight patrol vessels and 14 big-gun monitors. In addition, further patrolling was undertaken by a collection of armed drifter, trawlers and requisitioned yachts. Ships detached from the Harwich Force and the Dover Patrol formed a third force, based on Dunkirk, that patrolled the far side of the Channel.

Across the water, the advancing German armies had overrun much of the Belgian coast in 1914. A destroyer and U-boat base had been established at Bruges, inland, with canal exits to the sea at Zeebrugge and Ostend. Through these, U-boats managed to slip past or over the Channel nets and minefields which, it had been hoped, would deny them access to the open sea. With typical thoroughness, the Germans had protected their investment with numerous coastal defence batteries. As can be imagined, this was a very warm corner of the war at sea, with reciprocal bombardments, attacks by float planes, mining and small ship actions.

The tempo of activity increased after Jutland. With the High Seas Fleet now rusting quietly in its anchorages, there was little for its many escorting destroyers to do. However, it was essential for Scheer to give the impression that active operations were still undertaken. On 23 October he despatched no less than 24 destroyers to Zeebrugge under the flotillas' commodore, Captain Michelsen.

Admiral Bacon knew of their presence, but during the inky darkness of the night of 26/27 October, they slipped out of harbour. Michelsen's 3rd Flotilla surprised the drifters guarding the net between the Goodwin Sands and the Outer Ruytingen Banks, sinking seven and setting an eighth on fire. When a single British destroyer, *Flirt*, attempted to intervene, she too was sent to the bottom. The German 9th Flotilla entered the Straits where it sank the empty transport *Queen*, permitting her crew to escape in the boats. Returning to Zeebrugge, the flotilla became involved in a running fight with three British destroyers, blowing the bows off *Nubian* and scoring hits on *Amazon* and *Mohawk*. Michelsen could congratulate himself on carrying out a successful operation without loss. *Nubian* was towed into port safely and subsequently married to the bows of another Tribal Class destroyer, *Zulu*, the stern of which had been blown off by a mine. In this form the composite destroyer returned to the fray as HMS *Zubian*.

Coming on top of the Jutland casualties and the death of Field Marshal Lord Kitchener aboard the cruiser *Hampshire* when she was mined off the north coast of Scotland, this episode produced a wave of public dissatisfaction at the way the war at sea was being conducted. Arthur Balfour, the First Lord of the Admiralty, issued a politician's typically bland statement to the effect that if the raid was repeated 'it would be severely dealt with.' It was repeated on a smaller scale during the evening of 23 November, but the Germans retreated unharmed as soon as opposition was encountered. The press tartly reminded Balfour of his promise, echoing the public view that there seemed to be a sad lack of aggression in the upper echelons of the Navy.

There was certainly no lack of it further down the chain of command. As luck would have it two U-boats, *U-20* and *U-30*, ran aground in the fog off the west coast of Jutland. Scheer despatched a half-flotilla of destroyers to rescue them, covered by no less than four dreadnoughts and the battle cruiser *Moltke*. Only *U-30* could be recovered and, while returning to base on 5 November, the German ships ran close to the patrolling British submarine *J-1*, commanded by Commander Noel Lawrence, a veteran of the successful British submarine campaign in the Baltic. Lawrence spotted them through his periscope at a range of 4,000 yards. Although a heavy swell was running, it was decided to attack. At one point *J-1*'s bows broke the surface, fortunately without attracting the attention of the enemy lookouts. Lawrence dived, running his motors hard, and at that moment the four German battleships entered his sights. Doing a rapid calculation, he fired his four bow tubes with a spread of five degrees, then took *J-1* down to rest on the sea bed. There was silence in the control room while the range was counted off. There was a distant boom, then another, followed by cheering throughout the boat. One torpedo had hit the *Kronprinz Wilhelm* and another had found a home in the *Grosser Kurfurst*, both of which would spend months in dock. To have torpedoed one battleship during a patrol was a considerable achievement, but to have torpedoed two was almost beyond belief. Lawrence later commented that he wished he had fired at a single ship and sent her to the bottom, but had been reasonably certain that he could account for two. The Kaiser flew into one of his rages and gave Scheer the benefit of his wide experience: 'To risk a squadron, and by so doing nearly risk the loss of two armoured ships in order to save two U-boats, is disproportionate and must not be attempted again!'

Ostensibly, 1917 began well for the Allies. Germany resumed unrestricted submarine warfare, having calculated that this would probably bring the United States into the war on the side of the Allies, without being able to contribute anything significant in either the military or naval spheres for the next two years, a calculation that proved to be flawed. On 13 March American merchantmen bound for the war zones were defensively armed, and on 6 April America declared war on Germany. Against this, Russia collapsed into revolution and civil war, enabling the Central Powers to transfer large numbers of troops from the Eastern to the Western Fronts, while the French Army was beginning to show signs of exhaustion.

By now, Jellicoe had reached the top of his profession and become First Sea Lord. Beatty took over as commander of the Grand Fleet, an appointment welcomed by many who believed that he was more of a fighter than his predecessor and would bring on the decisive battle everyone had hoped for. In fact the only decisive battle being fought at sea was being won by the U-boats. Even Scheer had now been converted to the view that the High Seas Fleet existed solely to safeguard the U-boats' return to base. The recently appointed German Chief of Naval Staff, Admiral Henning von Holtzendorff, calculated that if 600,000 tons of Allied shipping could be sunk every month and 40% of neutral shipping persuaded not to enter British ports, then Britain would be forced out of the war within five months. Jellicoe reached a similar conclusion, predicting that unless the U-boat menace could be brought under control, the United Kingdom's supplies of food and vital raw materials would run out by July. Yet, he stubbornly refused to alter the official Admiralty view that as long as the main trade routes were patrolled, only troop and coal convoys required escorts. With monthly losses actually exceeding those considered necessary for a British defeat by Holtzendorff, the situation became desperate. Under intense pressure from Prime Minister Lloyd George, Beatty and the Americans, the Admiralty finally gave way. The effect was magical. U-boats began to find difficulty in making their attacks and Allied losses dropped dramatically. Suddenly, U-boats encountered much strengthened defences in the Straits of Dover and were unable to make their usual night passage save at terrible risk. They therefore had to burn valuable fuel making the passage round the north of Scotland, which clearly reduced the amount of time they could spend on patrol. They also had to face the depth charge, a new and very dangerous weapon they were not aware of until May 1917, although it had been used in small quantities for ten months. British destroyers which had been used to idling their time away with the Grand Fleet now found themselves back in the war and being reinforced by American warships.

Although the battle against the U-boats took place mainly in the outer reaches of the Channel and the Western Approaches to the United Kingdom, there was still fighting in the North Sea. Having received intelligence that more German destroyers were being despatched to Zeebrugge during the evening of 22 January, the Admiralty ordered Tyrwhitt to intercept them. Leaving Harwich at 17:30 with six light cruisers, two flotilla leaders and 16 destroyers, by midnight he had deployed his force across all the likely approach routes. The German force, consisting of one flotilla leader and ten destroyers, was led by Commander Max Schultz. At 02:45 they ran into some of Tyrwhitt's cruisers, which promptly opened fire. *V69*, Schutlz's flotilla leader, struck by a shell that temporarily jammed her steering, smashed into another destroyer, *G41*. The remainder headed directly for Zeebrugge, concealed by a dense smoke screen.

At 03:40 *V69* ran into several more British cruisers and received such a battering that his opponents thought she had sunk, although she managed to limp off in the direction of the Dutch coast. Despite the rip in her side, *G41* managed to get into Zeebrugge. A third destroyer, *S50*, had become separated and was straggling towards the base when she ran into several British destroyers with whom she engaged in a spirited gunnery duel. Finally, after slamming a torpedo into the destroyer *Simoom*, she escaped and made her way back to Germany. By dawn, the action had clearly ended and, after sinking the crippled *Simoom*, Tyrwhitt's force returned home, less than satisfied by the night's work.

At last light on 25/26 February, Commander Tillesen left Zeebrugge with six destroyers to attack Dover while a further five under Commander Albrecht headed for the Downs anchorage, hoping to create mayhem among the merchantmen waiting to enter the Thames. Neither group managed to complete its mission. At 22:30, the destroyer *Laverock*, commanded by Lieutenant Binmore, was patrolling above the central portion of the anti-submarine mine barrage when Tillesen's ships came into view. *Laverock* was hit several times, but by manoeuvring cleverly and opening fire from different positions, Binmore managed to convince Tillesen that he was dealing with three ships and he turned for home in the belief that heavy British reinforcements were on their way. Albrecht did very little better, managing only to bang a few shells into Margate, Westgate and the North Foreland radio station before shearing off.

It was unfortunate that the poor results of this raid induced a sense of complacency both at Dover and in the Admiralty. In March, Bacon was warned that another raid was in the offing, he did not think it necessary to strengthen the mid-Channel patrol, which consisted of just four destroyers and relied on reinforcements that would be despatched from Dover or Deal. Tillesen left Zeebrugge during the evening of 17 March with two flotillas. The 6th, with seven destroyers, would cross the central area of the barrage while five vessels of Z Flotilla, under Albrecht, crossed some way to the east. At this point the remaining four destroyers of Z Flotilla, under Lieutenant Commander Zandler, was to attack shipping in the Downs.

A little before 23:00 Tillesen's flotilla encountered the small pre-war destroyer *Paragon*. Taken completely by surprise and hopelessly outnumbered, she was quickly battered into a burning wreck by concentrated gunfire and given her *coup de grace* by a torpedo. At this point the flames reached her

117

depth charges. The resulting explosion tore the ship in half. Two more British destroyers, *Llewellyn* and *Laferey*, closed in to investigate the firing, but in the intense darkness neither saw their opponents. *Llewellyn* was quickly crippled by a torpedo and then the Germans, still unseen, returned to base. A search for *Paragon*'s survivors succeeded in rescuing just ten of her 75-strong crew.

Meanwhile, following the torpedoing of *Llewellyn*, Admiral Bacon was informed that U-boats were apparently active in the area. He recalled the Dover destroyers, which had just put to sea, but no sooner had they dropped anchor than the German destroyers had sunk a drifter near the Downs and shelled both Broadstairs and Ramsgate. These were Zandler's ships, and by the time the Deal destroyers had been scrambled to drive them off they had gone.

On the night of 20 April the Germans attempted to repeat their success with their 3rd Destroyer Flotilla. As usual, four British destroyers were patrolling the barrage but in addition to destroyer leaders, *Swift* and *Broke*, had been sent to cover the area south-west of the Goodwin Sands. Unexpectedly, they came into contact with six German destroyers, on their way to bombard Dover. A fierce melee ensued, involving one of the most remarkable incidents in British naval history. *Swift* and *Broke*, commanded respectively by Commmander A.M. Peck and Commander E.R.G. Evans, the latter a survivor of Captain Robert Scott's tragic expedition to the South Pole, charged straight in among the Germans, guns blazing. *Swift* sustained some damage but, undeterred, Peck tried to ram an enemy destroyer. His night vision destroyed by gun flashes, he missed but passed clean through the enemy line, simultaneously causing a major explosion aboard one of the German vessels with a direct hit from one of his torpedoes.

Evans rammed *Broke* into the enemy's *G-42*, driving his bows deep into his opponent by running his engines at full power. Germans tried to scramble over *Broke*'s bows. Following a shout of 'Repel boarders!' (not heard aboard a

118

British warship for many a long year) a midshipman raced forward with a party of seamen armed with cutlasses, rifles and bayonets, iron bars and even meat cleavers. Leading Seaman Ingleson distinguished himself with his rifle and bayonet, but another burley seaman took the matter so seriously that, when confronted by a German petty officer scrambling aboard, he transferred his cutlass from right hand to left and landed a tremendous punch between the man's eyes, sending him tumbling back onto his own ship. *Broke*'s guns were also firing into *G-42* at point-blank range as she drove the German onto her beam ends.

The retreating enemy survivors opened fire on both ships impartially, aggravating a fire that had broken out aboard *Broke*. With a shriek of tearing metal, Evans reversed her out of his victim and tried to join *Swift*, which was chasing the enemy, but both British destroyers were now so severely damaged that they lacked the necessary speed. While limping back to Dover, Evans passed the sinking *G-42* and then came across *G-48*, the destroyer torpedoed by *Swift* early in the action. The German was sinking and on fire but surrender was not on her captain's mind as she fired a single shell, hitting *Broke*'s bridge. At this point *Broke*'s engines stopped and she began to drift down towards her burning opponent. For a while there was a real danger that the enemy's magazine would explode as the flames spread, destroying both ships in the explosion, but in the nick of time the engine room staff managed to produce sufficient power to move her out of immediate danger and *G-48* sank. Help arrived in due course, enabling *Broke* to be towed into harbour by another destroyer, but *Swift* managed to get in under her own steam. Some 40 of *Broke*'s crew had been killed or wounded, while *Swift* lost a further five. In an era of grim, industrial slaughter, this was just the sort of victory over odds to raise spirits. Understandably, Evans became a national hero overnight.

The incident provided a sharp lesson for the senior German naval officers based at Zeebrugge. A few shells lobbed into a sleeping coastal town were hardly worth the loss of two destroyers. Attacks into the Channel and Downs areas ceased, although a raid on Dunkirk sank a French destroyer. Nevertheless, Admiral Bacon decided that Zeebrugge had become a nest of snakes that had to be cleaned out. On 12 May no less than 41 warships of various types sailed from Dover and Harwich to deliver an 85-minute bombardment. The stars of the show were three monitors with 15-inch guns that were to shell the lock gates from a distance of 13 miles. Their shooting was remarkably good, for although the gates themselves were undamaged, no less than 19 shells landed within 15 yards of them.

Next, Ostend was bombarded on 4 June. Only two monitors were involved, landing 20 shells in the dockyard area, damaging several destroyers and sinking some smaller craft. Elements of the Harwich Force became involved with two German destroyers, one of which, *S-20*, was sunk while the other was chased back into Zeebrugge. Subsequently, a monitor and covering force were allocated to bombard Zeebrugge and Ostend whenever wind and tidal conditions permitted. At one stage the War Cabinet approved a plan for the Army in Flanders to capture the Belgian coast in conjunction with a an amphibious operation that would put no less than 24,000 men ashore, but this remained still-born when priority was given to Field Marshal Haig's Passchendaele offensive.

A further offensive move was the blocking of a loophole in the British blockade of Germany. German merchant ships were hugging their own coast and that of neutral Holland to collect cargos from the port of Rotterdam. On 17 July destroyers of the Harwich Force put a stop to this trade by sinking two enemy merchant vessels and capturing four more during their coastal passage.

A second foray, known as the Second Battle of Heligoland Bight in Germany but rarely mentioned in British histories, produced less satisfactory results. On 17 November a force consisting of the battle cruisers *Tiger, Renown, Repulse,*

Courageous and *Glorious*, the cruisers *Calypso* and *Caledon*, plus escorting destroyers, entered the Bight. In command was Admiral Sir Charles Napier, whose intention was to disrupt the activities of German minesweepers attempting to clear existing British minefields. Apart from the enemy's minesweepers and a patrol craft, the *Kedingen*, which was hastily abandoned by her crew and captured, the Admiral Ludwig von Reuter's covering force consisted of two battleships, *Kaiser* and *Kaiserin*, plus a cruiser and destroyers. During a brief exchange of fire, *Kaiserin* scored a direct hit on *Calypso*'s bridge, killing everyone present, and *Repulse* hit the cruiser *Konigsberg*, starting a fire. The Germans then retired behind their own minefields, ending the action.

In his memoirs, Admiral Scheer expresses great interest in the two British cruisers, which had only recently entered service. His admired their great speed, which he estimated at 33 knots although 30 knots was the official figure. He believed that one of them was responsible for hitting the *Konigsberg*, commenting that during its descent the British shell 'passed through all three funnels of the ship, went through the upper deck into a coal bunker against the inner wall of which it burst, causing a fire. The fragments of this shell were picked up and its calibre determined. This proved to us that the English had built a new class of cruiser armed with a 38 cm gun.' In fact the main armament of this class of cruiser was 5×6-inch guns, while that of the *Repulse* was 6×15-inch (i.e. 38 cm) guns. As his memoirs were written some years after the event and probably compiled from notes written at the time, this probably explains why the Admiral allowed the mistake to stand.

Meanwhile, the German Naval Command had become aware that British convoys between Lerwick and Bergen in neutral Norway were only lightly escorted. These convoys were extremely important as they exported manufactured goods and imported vital iron ore from Sweden and timber pit props from all over Scandinavia. Two light cruisers, the *Bremse* and the *Brummer*, were considered ideal for the task of disrupting them. Originally laid down in the Vulcan Yard in Stettin for service as fast minelayers with the Imperial Russian Navy, they were taken into German service on completion in 1916. They could be coal or oil fired and were capable of a maximum speed of 28 knots. Their main armament consisted of 4 × 5.9-inch guns and they possessed the capacity to carry 400 mines as deck cargo.

Shortly before dawn on 17 October they had encountered a convoy of twelve merchantmen escorted by two destroyers and two armed trawlers. One destroyer, *Strongbow*, attacked at once but was sunk within minutes, as was the second, *Mary Rose*, when she attacked. The cruisers then set about the merchantmen at will, only three of them and the two trawlers being able to make their escape. As many of the ships were neutrals, the incident naturally provoked protests. Scheer's memoirs contain the universal German reaction to these. 'If England wanted to demand the right to enjoy undisturbed supplies, thanks to the compliance of the neutrals, or the pressure brought to bear on them, no one could expect us to look on with folded hands until English sea power had completed its work of destroying our nation by starvation. The counter-measures which this necessitated must recoil upon England as the originator of this form of warfare.'

On 12 December a half-flotilla of German destroyers under Commander Heinecke attacked shipping in the swept channel off the Northumbrian coast, sinking one merchant vessel of 5,000 tons and two smaller craft. On the same day a second half-flotilla, consisting of four destroyers under Lieutenant Commander Hans Holbe, steamed due north in heavy weather and encountered a British convoy, consisting of six merchant ships escorted by two destroyers and four armed trawlers, off Bergen. One of the British destroyers, *Partridge*, fought until her guns were out of action and she had been immobilised. In a final act of defiance before she went down, she launched a torpedo that struck the German *V-100* but did not explode. With the exception of the damaged destroyer *Pellew*, which escaped into a rain squall, the entire convoy and the rest of its escort were sunk.

Nothing was more certain than that the Germans would try to repeat these comparatively minor successes. As they had taken place within the Grand Fleet's area of responsibility, Beatty was forced to react. In future, a squadron of battleships would accompany each convoy, a provision that became easier with the arrival of an American battleship squadron under Admiral Sims, and the sailing dates of convoys became irregular.

The year 1917 therefore ended without either side achieving a clear-cut major success at sea. Within the Admiralty, too, there had been conflict of a different kind. Vice Admiral Bacon was a difficult man who ignored advice and paid brief attention to instructions. He shared a mutual antipathy with Rear Admiral Roger Keyes, the Director of the Admiralty Plans Division. He might claim, with some justice, that during his three years of command some 88,000 vessels had passed safely through the Channel, while only six had been lost to enemy action, but the fact was that U-boats had made free use of it and the Straits until the recent defensive measures had been imposed. He was supported by his old friend Jellicoe, but the latter had lost favour because of Napier's lack of success in the Heligoland Bight and the loss of the two Scandinavian convoys. The general opinion, shared by Prime Minister Lloyd George, was that Jellicoe and Bacon were too cautious to be effective. During the last week of December, Jellicoe was sent into retirement, being replaced by Admiral Sir Rosslyn Wemyss, while Rear Admiral Roger Keyes replaced Bacon at Dover.

CHAPTER 13

End Game – The Zeebrugge and Ostend Raids

By the Spring of 1918 the great movement of German troops from the now defunct Eastern Front to Western Europe was complete. Millions of rounds of artillery ammunition, both gas and high explosive, had been stockpiled close to the guns they would feed, targets had been registered and fire-plans constructed. The best soldiers had been formed into Storm Troop battalions that would lead the great offensives that would result in final victory for Germany in what was called the *Kaiserschlacht*, or Emperor's Battle. Failure in this huge undertaking, which must be completed before the American armies took the field in strength, could not be contemplated for one minute.

The first offensive lasted from 21 March until 5 April and struck the British Third and Fifth Armies. The Allied line was pushed back some 40 miles but held, at great cost. The second offensive was directed at the British Second Army in Flanders between 9 and 21 April. Some ground was lost but, once again, the line held. The third offensive struck the French Sixth Army on the Chemin des Dames sector on 27 May and by 4 June had carved out a salient 30 miles wide and 20 miles deep. The fighting was notable for the stubborn defence and counter-attacks made by American divisions, committed to action on the Western Front for the first time. Two further offensives, mounted between 9 and 13 June and 15 and 19 July, attempted to expand the ground gained but had little success. By then, most of the elite Storm Troop battalions had been decimated repeatedly and the remainder of the Army was of lesser quality. Despite the horrific losses that had been incurred, the promised victory had not materialised. Disappointment, disillusion and demoralisation began to spread throughout the German armies.

Scheer was at a loss to know how the Imperial Navy could help. He was aware that the British had heavily reinforced the escorts for convoys carrying reinforcements across the Channel and believed that a strike by the greater part of the High Seas Fleet against the Scandinavian convoys would result in the transfer of British warships to the north, leaving their cross-Channel troop transports vulnerable to destroyer and U-boat attack. At best, the plan was based on optimism, for while it was known that a battleship squadron now protected the Scandinavian convoys, the sailing dates of the convoys were not known.

The fleet put to sea at 06:00 on 23 April. Fog caused some delay but cleared during the day and the night passed without incident. The next morning dawned fine and clear, giving rise to hopes of a successful operation. However, shortly before 08:00 all hell broke loose when *Moltke*'s starboard inner propeller dropped off. The shaft raced in its bearings and the turbine, spinning out of control, began to scream. Vibration shattered the control wheel. Fragments of flying metal punctured the auxiliary condenser's discharge pipe, a number of steam exhaust pipes and the deck adjacent to the main switch room. As a result of this the central engine room and switch room were quickly flooded and the wing engine room began to take in water. Sea water penetrated the boilers, power declined and the engines gradually slowed to a stop. No less than 2,000 tons of water were shipped before a diver was put over the side to close the auxiliary condenser's water inlet and outlet valves.

A signal was despatched to Scheer reporting the battle cruiser's severe damage, her current speed of four knots and her position as being 40 sea miles west-south-west of Stavanger. The nearest ship, the light cruiser *Strassburg*, was despatched to her assistance immediately, followed by the battleship *Oldenburg* with instructions to tow the cripple. By 11:45 it was decided that she would return to base via the Bight.

There was no sign whatever of the Allied convoy but at 14:00 Scheer received a signal from Naval Staff containing details of the Scandinavian convoys' arrival and departure date. To the Admiral's chagrin, he learned that a convoy from England had reached Norway safely the previous day. All of these details could have been obtained without difficulty through the consular service in Norway and the fact that they had not simply confirms the compartmental thinking common in German military and naval circles. In the circumstances no alternative remained but to return to base.

At 20:30 *Oldenburg*'s towing cable snapped, resulting in an hour's delay before it could be made secure again. Hard work throughout the night had rewarded *Moltke* with some power, enabling her to proceed at 15 knots. At 07:50, while still some 40 nautical miles north of Heligoland, the returning ships were spotted by Lieutenant Allen, commanding the submarine *E42*. He launched a spread of four torpedoes, one of which headed straight for *Moltke*. The battle cruiser took evasive action but was hit amidships on her port side. Despite this she was able to enter the Jade under her own power. The minesweeper *M-27*, however, was not so lucky and sank after striking a German mine. With dry German humour, Scheer commented: 'Unfortunately the expedition did not meet with the success hoped for.'

Hardly had his ships come to anchor than he received a disquieting piece of news. The British had mounted a heavy amphibious raid on Zeebrugge. They had inflicted casualties and damage and, for the moment, the canal leading to the Bruges base was closed by sunken blockships. A similar raid on Ostend had been repulsed.

This was the work of Roger Keyes, now promoted to Vice Admiral. He was determined to eliminate the German U-boat bases and thereby force the enemy's submarines to operate from Germany itself and make the long passage round the north of Scotland to reach their operational area. This would also mean that the time the U-boats spent on patrol was reduced because of the additional consumption of fuel needed.

Keyes' plan for the attack on Zeebrugge was simple and broken down into five phases. In the first, the coast defence batteries would be bombarded by 15-inch monitors for several consecutive nights until the Germans began to believe that this had become a matter of routine. The second would involve the concealment of the approaching raiders by a dense smoke screen. The third required the guns on the harbour mole be neutralised by landing parties that would stream over its outer parapet into the heart of the defences from a suitably prepared assault ship. The fourth was designed to prevent enemy reinforcements entering the mole by blowing up the steel viaduct connecting it with the shore. Finally, blockships would enter the harbour and scuttle themselves inside the Bruges canal, their crews being taken off by coastal motor boats.

Straightforward though this might seem, a great deal of detailed preparation was required. A smokescreen of the necessary density, to be laid by coastal motor boats and motor launches, was produced by Wing Commander F.A. Brock, a member of the famous fireworks manufacturing family that had already producing suitable ammunition for dealing with

Zeppelin airships. The old cruiser *Vindictive* was chosen as the assault ship. It was decided that her port side would be brought against the outer side of the mole. A false upper deck was constructed from which the troops would cross the wall by means of 18 hinged gangways or brows, the vessel itself being secured to the parapet by grappling irons fore and aft. An 11-inch howitzer was mounted on the quarterdeck, plus one 7.5-inch on the foredeck and another on the false upper deck. Support for the infantry assault would be provided by three heavy and 16 light machine guns, some of the latter being mounted in an enlarged foremast fighting top, plus mortars and two flamethrowers. Wherever possible, additional protection was provided by draped splinter mats. There was a suspicion that the seaward approach to the mole was protected by a shallow minefield, so back-up for *Vindictive* was provided by two requisitioned Mersey ferries, *Daffodil* and *Iris*, which possessed double hulls and sufficiently powerful engines to cope with the strong tides of their home port. If necessary, they would land troops by my means of ladders. In the event of *Vindictive* reaching the mole safely, *Daffodil* had the task of pushing her hard against it with her bows for as long as necessary. The landing party would consist of the recently formed 4th Battalion Royal Marines, 200 seamen who had received infantry training and a further 50 seamen trained in demolition techniques.

The steel viaduct was to be destroyed by two obsolete submarines, *C-1* and *C-3*, the bows of which were packed with five tons of high explosive. *C-3* was to carry out the task, while *C-1* stood by to complete it if necessary. The blockships selected were five obsolete light cruisers, *Thetis*, *Intrepid* and *Iphigenia* at Zeebrugge and *Brilliant* and *Sirius* at Ostend. They were fitted with scuttling charges and additional ballast and each retained three of her guns, protected by half-inch steel shields. Duplicate steering and control stations were added and protected by splinter mats. Finally,

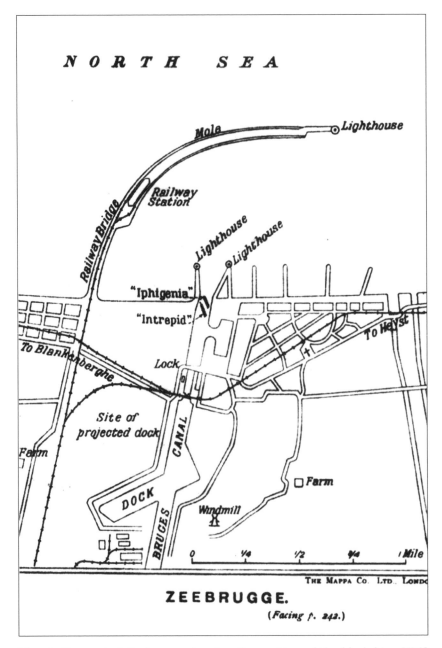

Map 6. The port of Zeebrugge showing the position of the blockships HMS *Intrepid* and HMS *Iphigenia*.

130

masts were removed and smoke generators fitted to conceal the escape of their crews.

The raiding force began its short passage at 17:00 on 22 April. As it approached Zeebrugge the motor launches and CMBs surged ahead, creating a dense fog with their smoke generators. For a while, this drifted towards the land at the same speed as the ships. Then, shortly before midnight, it backed, exposing the approaching force to full view. *Vindictive*, now fully exposed in the glare of searchlights, became the target of every German gun that would bear. Her commander, Captain Alfred Carpenter, realising that he must gain the shelter of the mole as quickly as possible, rang down for Full Ahead and completed the last few hundred yards of the run in at speed, grinding to a halt along the outer wall. *Daffodil*, her captain wounded by a shell exploding on the bridge, arrived from astern and pushed the cruiser hard against the wall while *Iris* closed in on the mole a little ahead.

It was unfortunate that *Vindictive*'s speed had taken her 300 yards past the point at which the troops were to have been put ashore directly into the interior of the enemy's defended zone at the seaward end of the mole. Again, so heavy had been the German fire that only two of the gangways had survived. Nevertheless, the troops swarmed across these and commenced their attack on the defended zone, losing heavily as they covered the additional distance despite covering fire being given from the cruiser's fighting top until it was wrecked by shellfire. Fierce hand-to-hand fighting took place in which the enemy also sustained losses.

Now was the moment for *C-3* to make her attack. At full speed her commander, Lieutenant Richard Sandford, drove her at the girders of the viaduct. One hundred yards short of the target he ordered his crew up into the conning tower and steered the little submarine in among the stanchions himself until, to the accompaniment of the scream of grinding metal, she came to a halt. While his crew launched a motor skiff he set the charge with great care. As the skiff shoved off, the water round it was flayed by rifle and machine gun fire. It was lucky that darkness and smoke made it impossible for the enemy to aim properly, as the skiff's engine failed to start and the crew were having to resort to the oars. Most received some sort of wound and Sandford was hit twice. Twelve minutes after *C-3* had been abandoned, her charges exploded, blowing the submarine and a large section of the viaduct skywards. No reinforcements could now reach those Germans defending the mole. Freed from their tormentors, the crew of the skiff rowed on until they were picked up by a picket boat which, by coincidence, was commanded by Sandford's elder brother, Francis.

The German gunners and naval infantrymen holding the seaward end of the mole had their hands fully occupied with the landing party and were unable to pay much attention to the approach of the three blockships. *Thetis*, under Commander F. Sneyd, in the lead, was hit several times but diverted the enemy's attention from *Intrepid* and *Iphigenia*. However, thanks to the damage sustained by *Thetis* and the tidal set, she missed the gap in the net boom and ploughed into the mesh. With the net now tangled around her propellers, she was pulled to port and, taking in water, grounded 300 yards short of the canal entrance. She had, however, pulled the net with her and so widened the gap in the boom so that *Intrepid*, commanded by Lieutenant S.S. Bonham-Carter, passed through and into the canal, where her scuttling charges were blown. While his crew scrambled into the boats, Bonham-Carter activated the smoke generators that would cover their retreat. The dense fog created may have blinded the defenders, but it also blinded Lieutenant E.W. Billyard-Leake, commanding *Iphigenia*, which nearly struck the canal's western pier before entering the waterway. She nudged *Intrepid* slightly out of position, and was then scuttled and abandoned under cover of her own smoke generators. Next to arrive on this scene of sinking ships, dense smoke and gunfire was Motor Launch *282*, commanded by Lieutenant Percy Dean, a Royal Naval Volunteer Reserve officer. Aged forty, Dean might have been regarded as a little too old for this sort of rough-and-tumble, but he remained perfectly calm and in full control of events, transferring over 100 men from the blockships' boats to the launch's deck and rescuing men from the water, despite a steering failure and the enemy's fire. Leaving the harbour when his task was done, he later transferred his passengers to the destroyer *Warwick*, aboard which Keyes was controlling the operation.

At 00:50, with the blockships now in position, Captain Carpenter decided to recall the landing parties. As *Vindictive*'s siren had been shot away, the signal was sounded by *Daffodil* and *Iris*. For the next fifteen minutes marines and bluejackets tumbled aboard, carrying with them as many of the dead and wounded as they could. When it was clear that there was no one else to come, *Daffodil* assisted *Vindictive* away from the mole and, joined by *Iris*, the three ships headed for the open sea, making smoke as they did so. Most of the enemy's fire fell astern, but by the worst possible luck a random shell exploded aboard *Iris*, killing 75 of the men packed into what had formerly been her saloons.

In total, British casualties during the raid amounted to 160 killed, 28 mortally wounded, 383 wounded, 16 missing and 13 captured. The destroyer *North Star* had been sunk by the enemy's coast defence batteries, and Motor Launches *110* and *424* had also been lost. No accurate figures for German personnel losses exist. That they were lower is beyond doubt, but as the eminent historian Barrie Pitt points out in his own study of the operation, *Zeebrugge – Eleven VCs Before Breakfast*, there exists a school of historians willing to accept the 'official' German version of events which tends to dismiss the question of casualties altogether, despite serious inconsistencies in the narrative.

Nevertheless, the object of the operation was not to create a large butcher's bill for the enemy, but to deny him the use of the Zeebrugge exit from the Bruges naval base. For some time, the Germans could not even make a start on reopening the canal as the local dredger had been sunk beside the mole by a coastal motor boat during the fighting. This meant that the Bruges U-boats already at sea would have to return to more distant bases in Germany, ending their patrols prematurely. In the end it became necessary to widen the canal opposite the sunken blockships so that by dredging a channel through the silt under their sterns it was possible for a small coastal U-boat to be warped past the obstruction, but only at high tide. Those ocean-going U-boats and destroyers caught in Bruges at the time of the raid stayed there for the rest of the war. Even after hostilities ended it took a year to restore the canal to working order.

The results of the raid on Ostend were less than satisfactory. The raiders were relying on two buoys as navigational markers, but these had been moved. *Brilliant*, the leading blockship, emerged from the smokescreen to find herself brightly illuminated by the defenders' searchlights. Having relied on dead reckoning her captain, Commander A.E. Godsall, was temporarily blinded and on recovery found that he was some distance to the east of the canal entrance. Before the course could be corrected, *Brilliant* had run on to a sandbank. Godsall went astern but before his ship could free herself she was struck on the port quarter by *Sirius*, the second blockship, which had been severely damaged and was in a sinking condition, and forced further aground. All that remained was to blow the scuttling charges and take off the blockship crews into motor launches.

A second attempt was made on 9 May. *Vindictive*, now converted to the blockship role and commanded by Godsall, accompanied by an even more ancient cruiser, *Sappho*, which had been launched in 1891. Unfortunately, *Sappho's* antique engines gave so much trouble that she had to turn back. Prior to the attack itself, monitors would deliver a bombardment and heavy bombers would unload their cargos directly over the defences. On this occasion the usual dense fog created by the smokescreen was supplemented by a natural mist but Godsal, a fine navigator, brought the old cruiser precisely to the canal mouth. He had been about to swing her across the main channel when he was killed by a shell bursting on the bridge. Lieutenant Victor Crutchley, despite being wounded, tried to complete the manoeuvre but by then it was too late and *Vindictive* had run aground beside the channel. As they had done on previous occasions, the motor launches performed prodigies of courage rescuing the crew under heavy fire after the scuttling charges had taken effect.

If the raids on Ostend had not been the successes that had been hoped for, that on Zeebrugge was in the British naval tradition stretching back as far as Drake. It restored the public's confidence in the Royal Navy and the fact that it had taken place on St George's Day, the day of England's national saint, provided the icing on the cake. Despite the grim ordeal that the Army was undergoing on the Continent, victory once more seemed to be a possibility.

For the Germans Zeebrugge had the opposite effect. It was alarming that such an assault had been made into the flank of their major offensive, and if it had happened once it could happen again. It was also depressing that after four years of war, Great Britain was still capable of mounting such an operation. Were these the reasons that 'official' versions of doubtful veracity were prepared and later offered to foreign historians?

After the Zeebrugge and Ostend raids neither side mounted major operations in the North Sea. Elsewhere, the German offensives ran down and finally came to a halt. On 8 August the British launched a massive counter-offensive at Amiens, using hundreds of tanks. The German armies never recovered from the blow and thereafter retreated slowly but steadily towards their homeland. Those troops holding Ostend, Zeebrugge and the Belgian coast were forced to conform to the general movement and abandoned their bases. If the news from the front depressed those at home, the news from home depressed the troops at the front. Food shortages were reaching starvation proportions while wage and price inflation were creating widespread unrest. The promised victories had not materialised, and those who promised them were no longer trusted.

CHAPTER 14

Envoie – The End of the High Seas Fleet – Mutiny, Internment and Scuttling

On 14 November 1918 a light cruiser flying the Imperial German Naval ensign and a rear admiral's flag entered the Firth of Forth, receiving the curious stares of British service personnel and civilians alike. She was the *Konigsberg*, the replacement for the cruiser that had been destroyed in the Rufiji River during the war's early days. The spectators noted a handsome ship with two very tall masts, three funnels, the foremost of which was higher than the other two, and eight 5.9-inch guns. Having taken up a position close to *Queen Elizabeth*, Admiral Beatty's flagship, *Konigsberg* dropped anchor. Her admiral's barge was called away and rowed across to the British flagship, where Rear Admiral von Meurer and his small staff climbed the accommodation ladder, exchanged stiffly formal compliments with those waiting above, and were led below.

The Armistice ending the Great War had been signed three days earlier. Its provisions required the Imperial German Navy to hand over for internment under the supervision of the Royal Navy eleven dreadnought battleships, five battle cruisers, eight light cruisers, fifty destroyers and all its surviving U-boats. There was no question of Meurer negotiating any improvement on these terms; he was aboard *Queen Elizabeth* to receive orders from Beatty as to how they were to be implemented and returned to *Konigsberg* knowing that his service was to be totally and very publicly humiliated.

The seeds that had germinated into mutiny and revolution had been present for a while. It was not just the long periods of idleness that had followed Jutland, although they had contributed to the rot. In some respects the social structure of the Navy mirrored that of the Army. Deck officers tended to be drawn from the upper classes and looked down on engineering and technical officers. Likewise, seamen were drawn from the merchant service and the fishing fleet, while men in the engineering branch were recruited in the country's industrial areas. Promotion to petty officer tended to be awarded to regulars rather than conscripts. At sea, living conditions were crowded, to the extent that in harbour a proportion of crews were housed in barracks. The winter of 1917/18 became known as the 'turnip winter' as little else was available to eat and cooks became adept at serving the vegetable in various guises. Even in better times good food was in short supply and was not distributed fairly. On the mess decks, bread was baked from potato flour, while the officers enjoyed wheaten rolls, plus cakes on Sundays. One senior officer with a weakness for fried eggs had them cooked and carried to the wardroom along the mess decks, where the men may not have seen an egg for weeks. Naturally, such things were resented and did nothing to improve morale.

Having spent so much time in harbour, the seamen could see that the civilians were even worse off than they were. The influence of the Russian revolution began to spread throughout the mess decks, where the most commonly held opinion was that, since Germany's allies were collapsing round her and the Army had failed to win victory during the recent offensives, the war was a complete waste of time. Among those expressing this view most forcefully were those who had just returned from the Belgian coast.

At the beginning of August 1918 Scheer became Chief of Admiralty Staff and Hipper assumed command of the High Seas Fleet. Watching events, he recognised beyond doubt that the Army was being roundly beaten and would disintegrate before long. In October he planned one final sortie which would prove that the Navy was still a power to be reckoned with. Some, but by no means all, senior officers, supported the idea, which would involve an operation similar to those with which the war had begun. On the mess decks, however, the agitators spread the word among the seamen that they were being taken on a death ride for the sake of the Navy's honour, and that was something the seamen were simply not prepared to tolerate.

As the fleet began assembling at Schillig Roads on 27 October, serious acts of sabotage took place to prevent its sailing. These included the deliberate absence of stokers, the extinguishing of furnaces, the opening of water cocks and the jamming of capstans so that anchors could not be hoisted. By the evening of 29 October all the battleships and light cruisers were affected. Aboard the *Thuringen* and *Helgoland* the red flag of revolution was hoisted. Officers were simply told to stay out of the way. On 31 October naval infantry and smaller warships were called in to restore order. For a while there was a standoff and a serious risk that blood would be shed. Finally, those involved in the disturbance surrendered. Some 1,000 of them were arrested and marched off, weakening the crews to the extent that the fleet could not put to sea anyway.

On 3 November a demonstration by seamen, soldiers, workers and their wives took place in Kiel, demanding the release of the arrested men. The demonstration was followed by a march towards the city centre. Its progress was blocked by an officer's patrol which opened fire when the crowd refused to disperse, killing eight of the demonstrators and wounding 29. During the night of 4 November the seamen formed councils, disarmed their officers and took control of their ships and barracks. Professional political agitators arrived to organise them and during the next few days they spread across Germany, being welcomed wherever they went. At the top of their list of demands were the abdication of the Hohenzollerns and the release of their comrades.

In Berlin, law and order broke down. The Kaiser had left Potsdam for his headquarters at Spa in Belgium on 29 October and the situation in the capital had deteriorated steadily ever since. During the days that followed he seemed divorced from reality. Having been informed that the Army was not prepared to fight any longer, he suggested that after the armistice had been signed he would personally lead the troops back to Germany. When told that this was not an option he demanded confirmation from the generals commanding the various German armies along the front and was horrified when this was forthcoming. He finally accepted the inevitable when a telephone call from Berlin confirmed that revolution had broken out and that the Berlin garrison, including the Kaiser's favourite regiment, the Kaiser Alexander Garde Grenadier Regiment No. 1, had gone over to the revolutionaries and that his abdication had become essential if civil war was to be avoided. He replied that he would abdicate as Emperor of Germany but not as King of Prussia, but was told that this was not acceptable. On 10 November he signed a deed of abdication and left for exile in Holland the following day. It was one of history's greatest ironies that the fleet that he had brought into being, nurtured and protected should be the principal instrument that brought about his downfall.

The date for the fleet's internment was set for 21 November. Included in the orders given to Admiral Meurer by Beatty was that those ships involved would unload all their ammunition, remove the breech blocks and gun sights from their guns and render their central gunnery control equipment inoperable. These tasks were completed during the evening of 18 November and at noon the following day Meurer led his ships out on their last voyage across the North Sea.

The rendezvous with the Grand Fleet was to take place at 08:00 on 21 November at May Island off the Firth of Forth. Over 240 British warships and an American squadron were drawn up in lines through which the Germans would have to pass. The High Seas Fleet arrived exactly on time and was escorted to its temporary anchorage in the Forth. Throughout, the Allied crews remained at Action Stations with their guns trained on their former opponents. Inspection teams then boarded the German ships to verify that Admiral Meurer had carried out his orders. During the afternoon Beatty despatched a signal to Meurer: 'The German flag will be hauled down at sunset today and will not be hoisted again without permission.'

Starting on 23 November and continuing for the next four days units of the High Seas Fleet reached Scapa Flow and were directed to what would be their last anchorages. Only skeleton crews were permitted to remain aboard and in due course the remainder were taken back to Germany in liners. Elsewhere, U-boats entered Harwich in small groups before being despatched to the breaker's yard.

For the officers and men remaining at Scapa Flow a hard winter lay ahead, followed by months of boredom in which they were not allowed to set foot ashore. Denied up to date news, it appeared to them that the armistice would expire on 21 June 1919 and that the British would seize their ships. As internment differed from capture, Admiral von Reuter, commanding the Germans at the Flow, felt that he could not allow his country's warships to fall into British hands. Lacking the means to resist, he devised a plan in great secrecy to scuttle the ships simultaneously upon a given signal. No one bothered to tell him that the expiry of the armistice terms had been extended by two days. Consequently, at 10:40 on 21 June the signal was given. Having opened then smashed the sea cocks and hoisted their ensigns for the last time, the German crews took to their boats with their personal possessions while spectators around the anchorage watched in astonishment as over seventy warships began sinking simultaneously.

In due course the crews, having spent a period in prison camp, were repatriated. Attempts to salvage the sunken wrecks met with mixed success. In some cases they were raised and towed away for breaking; in others the technical difficulties involved were immense and salvage was not even attempted. The latter remain, rusting steadily away until their steel crumbles and mingles with the silt producing reddish stains on the bed of the Flow. That is all that remains of the High Seas Fleet, once the pride and joy of Wilhelm Hohenzollern.

Appendix – The Admirals

Fisher, John Arbuthnot, 1st Baron (1841–1920)

Admiral John Fisher was born into a service family and was a veteran of the Crimean War. An unconventional and sometimes difficult man, he was also a sound administrator and gifted with a high degree of professional foresight. He became First Sea Lord in 1904 and instituted a series of reforms which, while unpopular with the more conservative elements of the Royal Navy, resulted in a thoroughly modernised service by the time war broke out in 1914. He is best remembered for the introduction of the *Dreadnought*, an all big-gun battleship that revolutionized warship design, but was also responsible for introducing the battle cruiser, which carried a battleship's armament and a cruiser's speed but lacked much of a battleship's protection, and for recommending the general use of fuel oil in place of coal. He retired in 1910 but was recalled to duty in October 1914. He resigned again in May 1915 following disagreement with Winston Churchill, the then First Lord of the Admiralty, over the Dardenelles campaign, which he felt was absorbing too many naval assets. While he was not personally involved in the North Sea battles, the Royal Navy that fought them was his creation.

Jellicoe, John Rushworth, 1st Earl (1859–1935)

Prior to his achieving flag rank, Jellicoe had enjoyed an adventurous career from which he was, at times, lucky to emerge with his life. He had taken part in the 1882 landing in Egypt, survived the notorious collision between the battleships *Victoria* and *Camperdown* in 1895 as a result of which the former sank with heavy loss of life and, as a captain, was

143

seriously wounded during the Boxer Rebellion while serving with the international relief force attempting to relieve the besieged Legation Quarter in Peking. His particular skill lay in gunnery and in 1905 he was appointed Director of Naval Ordnance. As early as 1908 Fisher nominated him as the most suitable commander for the Grand Fleet in the event of war and he was appointed to this post on 4 August 1914. Churchill described him as the only man on either side who could have lost the war in an afternoon. Professionally, he has been criticised for being over-cautious, unwilling to delegate and needlessly concerned with comparatively minor matters. Disappointment that Jutland had not produced a second Trafalgar concealed the fact that he had achieved a strategic success that virtually reduced the High Seas Fleet to impotence for the rest of the war. He was removed from active command shortly after the battle and appointed First Sea Lord. While conscientious and hard working, he did not enjoy a happy working relationship with Prime Minister Lloyd George, who was disappointed by his lack of optimism. His reluctance to institute a system of escorted convoys contributed to heavy losses in British and Allied merchant ships and resulted in his being dismissed on 24 December 1917. However, this was considered to be somewhat over-harsh by many and the following month he was promoted to Admiral of the Fleet and raised to the peerage. His final years of public service were spent as Governor-General of New Zealand.

Beatty, David, 1871–1936, 1st Earl,
The son of a cavalry officer, David Beatty achieved flag rank at the early age of 39. He had commanded a river gunboat with distinction during Kitchener's Nile campaign against the dervishes in the Sudan and in 1900 saw further active service during the Boxer Rebellion in China. He developed what today would be called a personality cult, the most obvious aspect of which was the wearing of his cap at a rakish angle over his left eye. Nevertheless, he obviously

possessed great abilities and these led to his serving as Winston Churchill's naval secretary between 1911 and 1913. During that period he made a number of influential connections which assisted in his securing his appointment as the commander of the Grand Fleet's battle cruiser squadron, a task for which his offensively minded temperament was well suited. He fought successful actions at Heligoland Bight and Dogger Bank but at Jutland the loss of three of his battle cruisers led to his being accused of impetuosity, although the real fault lay in the ships' vulnerable design. More telling was the criticism that during the early stages of the engagement he failed to keep Jellicoe fully informed as to what was happening. Despite this, he fitted the general public's idea of a fighting admiral and was appointed commander of the Grand Fleet shortly after Jutland. Ironically, no further opportunities for action came his way, although in November 1918 he was able to supervise the internment of the German High Seas Fleet. His rewards included promotion to Admiral of the Fleet and the award of an earldom. He became First Sea Lord in 1921 and held this appointment until 1927.

Tirpitz, Alfred von (1849–1930)
Born in Kustrin, then part of Prussia, Tirpitz was the son of a civil servant. As soon as he was old enough he joined the tiny Prussian Navy as a cadet and in due course became head of the torpedo branch. In 1897 he was appointed Secretary of State of the Ministry of Marine, a post he held for over eighteen years. It was he who suggested that the prestige of the recently created German Empire demanded possession of a navy to rival that of Great Britain, a suggestion adopted with enthusiasm by Kaiser Wilhelm II, anxious to prove that he was every bit the leader of a world power as were his British relatives. The concept was disastrous on several counts. First, it initiated a naval construction race between Germany and the United Kingdom in which the former lagged behind with no prospect of

achieving parity. Second, it turned Great Britain into a probable enemy, without an adequate reason for doing so. Third, the creation of a new, modern navy was prohibitively expensive, absorbing funds and resources needed elsewhere, principally by the Imperial German Army. This led to considerable internal friction, but Tirpitz was a master of intrigue and invariably got his way, largely because he had the personal support of the Kaiser. Indeed, a dispute between Tirpitz and the Kaiser's brother Heinrich was neatly resolved when the latter was promoted sideways to a position where his opinions didn't count. Tirpitz reached the zenith of his career when, in 1911, he was promoted to the unique rank of Grand Admiral, a rank unheard of even in the British Royal Navy. However, as the storm clouds began to gather in 1914, the enormity of what he had done suddenly dawned on Tirpitz. His High Seas Fleet could not hope to defeat the much larger Royal Navy and Great Britain had reached an understanding with Germany's two most probable enemies, France and Russia. He argued against war, but in Imperial Germany it was the Army that had the real power to influence decisions of that kind. Too late, he became a convert to submarine warfare, but by now his influence with the Kaiser had begun to wane.

In March 1916 he threatened to resign and the Kaiser called his bluff. He dabbled in politics for a while without achieving anything of note and gradually disappeared from view. Despite his reputation of being the father of the German Navy, he never held a major command at sea and his overall influence on his country's affairs can be seen as being catastrophic.

Scheer, Reinhard, 1863–1928

Scheer's first name was actually Arthur, following a family tradition, but this does not seem to have been taken into general use. He entered the Imperial Navy in 1879 and progressed steadily in rank despite his middle class origins. On the outbreak of war in 1914 he commanded in succession the IInd and IIIrd Battle Squadrons and took over command of the High Seas Fleet in January 1916. He was known as a strict disciplinarian and was given the nickname of 'the man in the iron mask.' During the Battle of Jutland he inflicted greater loss on Jellicoe's Grand Fleet than he sustained and managed to bring most of his badly mauled command home, enabling the German propaganda machine to claim a victory. This earned him the award of the *Pour le Merite With Oakleaves* and ennoblement by the Kaiser, although he refused to add the ritual 'von' prefix to his surname. He was, however, fully aware that he had had a narrow escape and when he next took the High Seas Fleet to sea the inaccurate report of a Zeppelin that the Grand Fleet was also at sea and closing on him was sufficient to make him head for home. After this experience he came to the view that the only way to defeat the United Kingdom at sea was by means of unrestricted submarine warfare, a view which he persuaded the Kaiser to share. In August 1918 he left the High Seas Fleet to become Chief of Naval Staff. In 1928 he accepted an invitation from his old adversary Jellicoe to visit England but contracted a fatal illness before he could make the journey.

Franz Hipper, 1863–1932
A Bavarian by birth, Hipper joined the Navy in 1881 and, like Scheer, rose steadily in rank until in 1913 he was appointed commander of the High Seas Fleet's Scouting Force. With this he made several raids on the east coast of England with varying degrees of success. At Jutland he inflicted heavy losses on Beatty's Battle Cruiser Fleet. Although he was scornful of some previous awards granted him by the Kaiser, he accepted the *Pour le Merite* in recognition of his ships' part in the battle. He was also ennobled but declined to add the prefix 'von' to his name, although he did accept a knighthood from King Ludwig III of Bavaria. In August 1918 he took over the High Seas Fleet from Scheer. On occasion he could be impulsive and when Germany's

defeat became inevitable he planned to take out the fleet to fight one last battle in which it would undoubtedly have been defeated but, in his eyes, saved its honour. His seamen, already demoralised by inactivity, recognised that in practical terms such a gesture was meaningless, and mutinied rather than put to sea. The mutiny grew and spread into a full-scale revolution that destroyed Imperial Germany.

Bibliography

Archibald, E.H.H., *The Fighting Ship in the Royal Navy 897–1984*, Blandford, Poole, 1984

Bennett, Geoffrey, *Coronel and the Falklands*, Batsford, London, 1962

Bennett, Geoffrey, *The Battle of Jutland*, Batsford, London, 1964

Bennett, Geoffrey, *Naval Battles of the First World War*, Batsford, London, 1968

Brookes, Ewart, *Destroyer – The History of a Unique Breed of Warship*, Hutchinson, London, 1962

Buchan, John, *A History of the Great War, Vols 1–4*, Nelson, London, 1921

Gray, Edwin, *A Damned Un-English Weapon – The Story of British Submarine Warfare*, Seeley Service, London, 1971

Gray Edwin, *The Killing Time – The German U-boats 1914–1918*, Seeley Service, London, 1972

Foster, Joe, *The Guns of the North-East – Coastal Defences From the Tyne to the Humber*, Pen & Sword, Barnsley, 2004

Jones, James Hartington, Ed, *The German Attack on Scarborough, December 16, 1914*, Quoin, Huddersfield, 1989

Haythornthwaite, Philip J., *The World War One Source Book*, Arms & Armour, London, 1992

Lake, Deborah, *The Zeebrugge and Ostend Raids 1918*, Pen & Sword, Barnsley, 2002

Layman, R.D., *Naval Aviation in the First World War*, Chatham Publishing, London, 1996

H.M. Le Fleming, *Warships of World War I*, Ian Allan, London, 1961

Macintyre, Captain Donald, *Jutland*, Evans Brothers, London, 1957

Pitt, Barrie, *Zeebrugge – Eleven VCs Before Breakfast*, Cassell, London, 1958

Ruge, Friedrich, *Scapa Flow 1919*, Ian Allan, London, 1973

Stephenson, Charles, *Zeppelins: German Airships 1900–40*, Osprey, Oxford, 2004

Sutherland, Jonathan and Canwell, Diane, *Battle of Britain 1917 – The First Heavy Bomber Raids on England*, Pen and Sword, Barnsley, 2006

Tarrant, V.E., *Jutland – The German Perspective*, Arms & Armour, London, 1995

Taylor, Edmond, *The Fossil Monarchies*, Weidenfeld & Nicolson, London, 1963

Taylor, John C., *German Warships of World War I*, Ian Allan, London, 1969

Thomas, David A., *Battles and Honours of the Royal Navy*, Leo Cooper, Barnsley, 1998

Index

Index of Ships

British and Allied Ships
FNN *Mousquet*, 25
HMS *Aboukir*, 23
HMS *Ajax*, 37
HMS *Alcantara*, 74
HMS *Ambuscade*, 39
HMS *Andes*, 74
HMS *Antrim*, 37
Arabic, 5, 71
HMS *Argyll*, 37
HMS *Arethusa*, 20, 21
HMS *Audacious*, 24, 31
HMS *Aurora*, 64, 67
HMS *Barham*, 92
HMS *Black Prince*, 100
HMS *Blanche*, 37
HMS *Boadicea*, 37
HMS *Brilliant*, 129, 134
HMS *Broke*, 7, 118–119
HM CML 110, 133
HM CML 282, 133
HM CML 424, 133
HMS *Caledon*, 121
HMS *Calypso*, 121
HMS *Canopus*, 28
HMS *Centurion*, 37
HMS *Chester*, 97
HMS *Comus*, 74
HMS *Conqueror*, 37
HMS *Conquest*, 76
HMS *Courageous*, 121
HMS *Cressy*, 23
HMS *C-1*, 129
HMS *C-3*, 129, 131–132
HMS *C-7*, 34
HMS *C-9*, 55–56
HMS *Daffodil*, 129, 130, 133
HMS *Defence*, 97
HMS *Devonshire*, 37
HMS *Doon*, 33, 56
HMS *Dreadnought*, 13, 77, 143
HMS *Dublin*, 100
HMS *D-3*, 28
HMS *D-5*, 28
HMS *Empress*, 81
HMS *Engadine*, 81
HMS *E-9*, 23
HMS *E-10*, 28
HMS *E-11*, 58

HMS *E-42*, 127
HMS *Falmouth*, 104
HMS *Fearless*, 20, 21
HMS *Forward*, 33, 55, 56
HMS *Furious*, 88
HMS *Glasgow*, 28
HMS *Glorious*, 121
HMS *Good Hope*, 28
HMS *Halcyon*, 27, 28
HMS *Hampshire*, 5, 113
HMS *Hawke*, 23
HMS *Hermes*, 24
HMS *Hogue*, 23
HMS *Indefatigable*, 94, 95
HMS *Indomitable*, 20, 28, 96, 97, 96
HMS *Inflexible*, 28, 96
HMS *Intrepid*, 129, 132
HMS *Invincible*, 20, 28, 96, 97
HMS *Iphigenia*, 129, 132
HMS *Iris*, 129, 133
HMS *J-1*, 114
HMS *King George V*, 37
HMS *King Stephen*, 77–78
HMS *Lance*, 31
HMS *Laverock*, 117
HMS *Legion*, 31
HMS *Lennox*, 31
HMS *Leopard*, 27
HMS *Lion*, 20, 21, 37, 64, 65, 66, 67, 69, 94
HMS *Lively*, 27
HMS *Loyal*, 31
HMS *Lynx*, 39
Lusitania, 5, 71
HMS *Malaya*, 92
HMS *Mary Rose*, 122
HMS *Meteor*, 67
HMS *Monarch*, 37
HMS *Monmouth*, 28
HMS *Moy*, 33
HMS *Munster*, 74
HMS *Nestor*, 95
HMS *New Zealand*, 20, 37, 64, 65, 66, 94,
HMS *Nomad*, 95
HMS *North Star*, 133
HMS *Nottingham*, 104
HMS *Obedient*, 100

HMS *Onslow*, 97
HMS *Orion*, 37
HMS *Otranto*, 28
HMS *Paragon*, 117–118
HMS *Partridge*, 122
HMS *Pathfinder*, 23
HMS *Patrol*, 33, 40, 55, 56
HMS *Pegasus*, 25
HMS *Pellew*, 123
HMS *Princes Royal*, 20, 37, 64, 65, 66, 94
HMS *Queen Elizabeth*, 137–138
HMS *Queen Mary*, 37, 94, 95
HMS *Renown*, 120–121
HMS *Repulse*, 120–121
HMS *Riviera*, 81
HMS *Roxburgh*, 37
HMS *Sappho*, 134
HMS *Shark*, 41, 97–98
HMS *Simoom*, 116–117
HMS *Sirius*, 129,
HMS *Southampton*, 95, 100
HMS *Strongbow*, 122
HMS *Success*, 27
Sussex, 72
HMS *Swift*, 118–119
HMS *Test*, 33
HMS *Tipperary*, 100
HMS *Thetis*, 132
HMS *Ramsey*, 73
HMS *Tiger*, 64, 65 66, 69, 94, 120–121
HMS *Undaunted*, 31
HMS *Valiant*, 92
HMS *Vindictive*, 129, 130, 133, 134, 135
HMS *Warrior*, 97, 100
HMS *Warspite*, 92
HMS *Warwick*, 133
HMS *Waveney*, 33
IRN *Yemtschuk* (Zemchug), 25
HMS *Zubian*, 113

German Ships
SMS *Ariadne*, 21
SMS *Berlin* (AMC), 24, 31
SMS *Blucher*, 27, 35–36, 46, 50, 52, 53–54, 55, 63, 65, 66, 67, 68–69

INDEX

SMS *Bremse*, 121–122,

SMS *Brummer*, 121–122

SMS *Derfflinger*, 35, 46, 47, 48, 63, 65, 66, 94, 96, 97, 98, 103

SMS *Dresden*, 32

SMS *Elbing*, 97, 100

SMS *Emden*, 25–26

SMS *Frankfurt*, 77, 97

SMS *Frauenlob*. 20, 21, 100

SMS G-41, 77, 116

SMS G-42, 118–119

SMS G-48, 119

SMS *Gneisenau*, 26

SMS *Graudenz*, 27, 63,

SMS *Greif*, 73–74

SMS *Grosser Kurfurst*, 95, 98, 114

SMS *Hamburg*, 39

SMS *Hela*, 23

SMS *Helgoland*, 98, 139

SMS *Kaiser*, 121,

SMS *Kaiserin*, 121

SMS *Karlsruhe*, 33

SMS *Kedingen*, 121

SMS *Kolberg*, 21, 27, 46, 48, 63, 64

SMS *Koln*, 21

SMS *Konig*, 95, 96, 98

SMS *Konigsberg* (1), 25

SMS *Konigsberg* (2), 121, 137–138

SMS *Kronprinz Wilhelm*, 114

SMS *Lutzow*, 75, 94, 96, 98

SMS *Magdeburg*, 17, 37

SMS *Mainz*, 21, 22

SMS *Markgraf*, 95, 96, 98

SMS *Meteor*, 73

SMS *Moewe*, 73

SMS *Moltke*, 27, 35, 36–37, 46, 47, 50, 52, 53, 55, 63, 65, 94, 98, 126–127

SMS *Munchen*, 104

SMS M-27, 127

Rio Negro, 32

SMS *Oldenburg*, 127

SMS *Ostfriesland*, 100

SMS *Pillau*, 97

SMS *Pommern*, 99, 100

SMS *Posen*, 100

SMS *Roon*, 41

SMS *Rostock*, 63, 100

SMS *Seydlitz*, 26, 35, 38, 46, 50, 52, 54, 55, 63, 64, 65, 66, 68, 75, 94, 95, 96, 98, 100, 103

SMS *Scharnhorst*, 26

SMS *Schleswig-Holstein*, 99

SMS *Seeadler*, 73

SMS *Stettin*, 20, 21

SMS *Stralsund*, 21, 27, 28, 63, 64

SMS *Strassburg*, 21, 27, 38, 127

SMS S-33, 38

SMS S-35, 99

SMS S-50, 116–117

SMS *Thuringen*, 139

SMS *Von der Tann*, 27, 35, 46, 47, 48, 63, 82, 94, 96, 98

SMS V-27, 95

SMS V-29, 95

SMS V-69, 116

SMS V-122

SMS V-155, 38

SMS V-158, 39

SMS V-160, 39

SMS V.187, 20

SMS U-9, 23

SMS U-20, 114

SMS U-27, 24, 36, 46

SMS U-30, 114

SMS *Westfalen*, 104

SMS *Wiesbaden*, 97

SMS *Wolf*, 73

General Index

Albrecht, Commander, 117

Bacon, Vice Admiral Sir Francis, 112, 117, 118, 120, 123

Balfour, Arthur, 113

Beatty, Admiral Sir David, 20, 21, 28, 29, 37, 38, 39–40, 57, 58, 64, 65, 66–67, 68, 69, 92, 93, 94, 95, 96, 103, 115, 123, 137–138, 140–141, 144–145

Bergen, 121

Bethmann-Holweg, Theobald, Imperial Chancellor, 82

Billyard-Leake, Lieutenant E.W. 132

Binmore, 117

Boedecker, Rear Admiral, 75, 76

Bonham-Carter, Lieutenant S.S. 132

Brandenburger, Captain Ernst, 106

Breihaupt, Lt-Commander Joachim, 83–84

Broad Fourteens, the, 31

Brock, Wing Commander, F.A., 128

Brock incendiary machine gun ammunition, 85

Bruges, 112,

Buddecke, Lieutenant, 38

Carl, Lieutenant, 38–39

Carpenter, Captain Alfred, 131

Christian, Rear Admiral A.H., 20

Churchill, Winston, 22, 28–29, 60, 92

Coronel, Battle of, 28, 29

Cromarty, 37.

Crutchley, Lieutenant Victor, 135

Cuxhaven, 81–82

Denny, Mate George, 77, 78

Dering, Lieutenant C.L.Y., 55

Dogger Bank, 36, 37, 63, 68, battle of, 63–69, 71, 92

Dover Patrol, 112,

Eckermann, Rear Admiral, 63, 64, 68

Elbe River, 32, 81

Evans, Commander E.R.G., 118, 119

Evan-Thomas, Rear Admiral Hugh, 92, 94, 95

Falkland Islands, Battle of the, 32

Fisher, Admiral John Arbuthnot, 143

Firth of Forth, 141

Franz Ferdinand, Archduke, 14

Fraser, Lt-Commander, 45, 50

Friedrichshafen, 81

Gaudecker, Lt-Commander, 39

German heavy bomber offensive against England, 107

German heavy bomber losses, 108

Godsall, Commmander A.E., 134–135

Goodenough, Commodore W.R., 20, 21, 64

Goodwin Sands, 113,

Gotha heavy bombers, 106

Hartlepool, description and defences of, 33–34, bombardment of, 52–57,

Hartog, Captain, 96,

Harvey, Major Francis, 95

Harwich Force, 112,

151

Heinecke, Commander, 122
Heligoland Bight, 17, 37, 40, 120–121
Henry, Prince, of Prussia, 73
Hipper, Admiral Franz, 26, 27, 28, 29, 33, 36, 37, 38, 40, 41, 45–46, 50, 57–58, 59, 63, 64, 65, 67, 68, 69, 93, 94, 95, 96, 98, 101, 139, 147–148
Holb, Commander Hans, 122–123
Hoeppner, General Ernst von, 105, 106, 109
Holtzendorff, Admiral, Henning von, 115
Horton, Lieutenant Max, 23
Hull, 83
Ingenohl, Admiral Friedrich von, 15, 22, 25, 26, 31, 32, 33, 37, 39, 40, 41, 59, 64, 68,
Jade River, 21, 27, 32
Jellicoe, Admiral Sir John, 92, 94, 96, 98, 99, 102, 103, 104, 111, 115, 123, 143–144
Jutland, Battle of, 91–100
Kaiser Wilhelm II, 11–12, 14, 15, 22–23, 29, 41, 68, 82, 91, 103, 114, abdicates 140
Kaiserschlacht, 125–126
Keyes, Vice Admiral R.J.B., 17, 58, 123, 128
Kiel Canal, 13
Kiel mutiny, 139–140
King George V, 102
Kitchener, Lord, 59, 113
Knorr, Captain von, 73
Lawrence, Commander Noel, 114
Lerwick, 121,
Levetzow, Captain von, 55
Lloyd George, 115, 123
Loftus-Jones, Commander, 97–98
Lowestoft, 75–76, 77
Maas, Rear Admiral Leberecht, 21–22
Marix, Lieutenant R.G.L., 81
Martin, Captain William, 77, 78
Mathy, Lt-Commander Heinrich, 83, 87

Meurer, Rear Admiral Von, 137, 138, 140, 141
Michelsen, Captain, 113,
Moore, Rear Admiral A.G.H., 64, 65, 67, 68, 69
Naismith, Lt-Commander M.E., 58–59
Napier, Admiral Sir Charles, 121
Ostend, 112, 120, first raid on, 128–134, second raid on, 134–135
'Ostend Carrier Pigeon Battalion' 105, 107
Outer Ruytingen Banks, 113
Peck, Commander, A.M.,
Pelly, Captain H.B., 65
Phillips, Lieutenant Tom, 78
Pohl, Admiral Hugo von, 22, 23, 68, 72
Pomeroy explosive machine gun ammunition, 86
Raeder, Commander Erich, 46
Reuter, Admiral Ludwig von, 121
Robinson, Lieutenant William Leefe, 86–87
Robson, Lt-Colonel Lancelot, 44, 45, 52, 59, 60
Room 40, 17, 37, 103
Rosyth, 61
Sandford, Lieutenant Richard, 131–132
Scapa Flow, 37, 92, 112, 141, scuttlings at, 141–142
Scarborough, description of, 34–35, bombardment of, 46–48
Scheer, Admiral Reinhard, 72, 75, 86, 91, 94, 95, 96, 98–99, 101, 102–103, 104, 111, 113, 114, 115, 116, 121, 122, 126, 127, 128, 139, 146–147
Schillig Roads, 29, High Seas Fleet mutinies in, 139
Schultz, Commander Max, 116
Schutte-Lanz organisation, see Zeppelins
Scott, Admiral Sir Percy, 83
Scott, Captain Robert, 118
Sneyd, Commander F.,

Spee, Vice Admiral Maximilian Graf von, 26, 32
Strasser, Captain Peter, 86, 88
Sturdee, Vice Admiral Sir Doveton, 28
Terschelling, 76
Tempest, Lieutenant Wulstan J., 87
Tillesen, Commander, 117
Tirpitz, Admiral Alfred von, 12–14, 22, 41, 59, 68, 145–146
Tirpitz, Lieutenant von, 22
Trechmann, Captain Otto, 51, 54, 60
Trechmann, Lieutenant Richard, 51, 60
Tyrwhitt, Commodore, R.Y., 20, 21, 64, 75–76, 81, 82, 112, 116, 117
Wardle, Captain T.E., 74
Warneford, Sub-Lieutenant R.A.J., 84–85,
Warrender, Vice Admiral Sir George, 37, 40, 58,
Weddigen, Lieutenant Otto, 23
Wemyss, Admiral Sir Rosslyn, 123
Whitby, description of, 34, bombardment of, 48
Wilhelmshaven, 29
Yarmouth, 1st bombardment of, 26–27, 2nd bombardment of, 75, 77
Zandler, Lt-Commander, 117
Zeebrugge, 112, 113, 116, 117, 119, 120, raid on 128–134
Zeppelin, Count Ferdinand von, 79 80
Zeppelin bases, 80
Zeppelin losses, 89
Zeppelin offensive against England, 82–87, 91
Zeppelin and Schutte-Lanz airships: L3, 69. L4, 69. L5, 67, 82. L6, 82. L7, 75. L13, 83, 103. L15, 83–84. L19, 77. L21, 76, 87. L31, 87. L33, 87. L34, 87. L53, 88. L54, 88. L60, 88. L70, 88. Z9, 81. LZ37, 84–85. SL11, 86–87